LOUISA MAY ALCOTT

QUILTS OF HER LIFE, HER WORK, HER HEART

LOUISA MAY ALCOTT

QUILTS OF HER LIFE, HER WORK, HER HEART

By Terry Clothier Thompson

Editor: Kent Richards

Technical Editor: Shannon Richards

Book Design: Brian Grubb

Photography: Aaron T. Leimkuehler

Illustration: Lon Eric Craven

Production assistance: Jo Ann Groves

Photo Credits: Louisa May Alcott photos are from "Life, Letters and Journals – Louisa May Alcott." Orchard House photo on page 37 is from the Library of Congress Historic American Buildings Survey Frank O. Branzetti, Photographer April 7, 1941. All other photos are from the collection of Terry Clothier Thompson.

Published by:
Kansas City Star Books
1729 Grand Blvd.
Kansas City, Missouri, USA 64108

First edition, first printing 978-1-933466-53-8
Printed in the United States of America by
Walsworth Publishing Co., Marceline, MO

To order copies, call StarInfo at
(816) 234-4636 and say "Books."

www.PickleDish.com

KANSAS CITY STAR BOOKS
Kansas City, Missouri

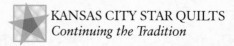

KANSAS CITY STAR QUILTS
Continuing the Tradition

PickleDish.com
The Quilter's Home Page

LOUISA MAY ALCOTT

QUILTS OF HER LIFE, HER WORK, HER HEART

By Terry Clothier Thompson

Why I designed the "Louisa" quilt

I grew up in the 1940's and 50's. Children played jacks, traded comic books, listened to the radio, and sat on the front porch playing card games. One of my favorites was "Authors." The game featured thirteen famous male authors and one famous female American author, Louisa May Alcott. I was impressed that she was placed with such famous writers and I always hoped I would draw her card first. Of course I had to read "Little Women" and I watched every movie ever made about Louisa and her family. When I became a mother, I would read her books to my daughter Shannon.

Three years ago I attended a local antique show and bought an old book titled "Life, Letters and Journals—Louisa M. Alcott." I opened the book to the first page on which the following dedication was written: "To— Mrs. Anna B. Pratt." Anna was the sole surviving sister of Louisa May Alcott, and her never failing help, comforter, and friend from birth to death. Anna gave Louisa's letters, (those that were not too personal), journals, and her mother and fathers early letters to Ednah Cheney to assemble into the book. The letters and notations begin in 1832 and end February 8, 1888.

Reading passages from her letters and journal showed me Louisa's character, thoughts and feelings. Her financial struggles and her self image inspired me to try to capture "cameos" of her life thru this story quilt of a storyteller. Each block portrays events in the lives of the Alcott family. Throughout "Louisa: Quilts of Her Life, Her Work, Her Heart" you will find passages taken from this inspiring book.

My intention for "Louisa: Quilts of Her Life, Her Work, Her Heart" is to combine history with the making of quilts. You might ask your quilt shop to hold classes, choose a book from the bibliography and take turns reading about Louisa's life as you sew. Form a special "Quilt and Book" club in your quilt guild, or home sewing groups, to include the historical content of 19th century quilt-making. The "Louisa" quilt itself is perfectly suited for a block-of-the-month project.

I believe knowing the facts of historical quilts makes the making of the quilt more meaningful. Encourage members of your group to bring old family letters, dresses, diaries, pictures, and needlework that will add interest and meaning to the social history of quilt making.

Acknowledgements

Jean Stanclift: appliqué

Lori Kukuk: machine quilting

Karalee Fisher: piecework

Rosie Mayhew: machine quilting

Kent Richards: preparing pattern pieces for appliqué

Thanks to all of these talented people for their fine work and contributions to this book.

Table of Contents

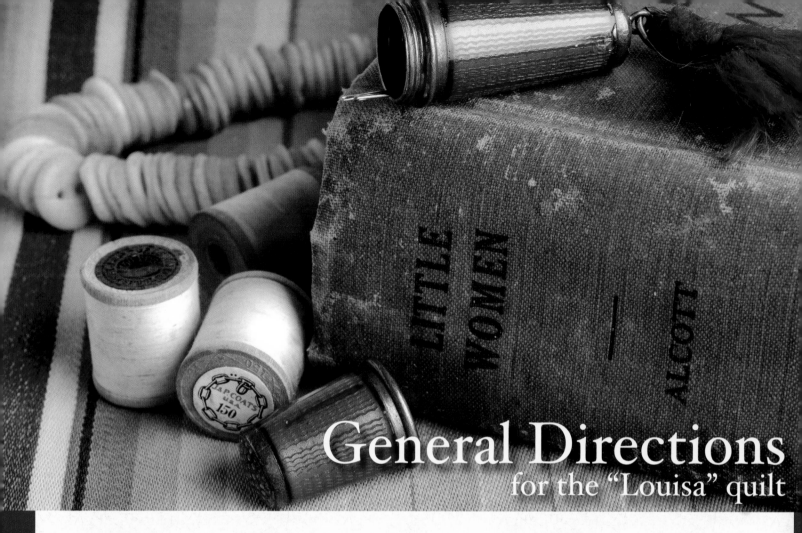

General Directions
for the "Louisa" quilt

There are 9 appliquéd octagon blocks and 6 pieced blocks. Each block tells the story of the life and times of Louisa and her family before and during the Civil War. Yardages for the appliquéd blocks are provided in the block directions. Our patterns use a variety of different fabrics: calico, floral and stripes, woven plaids and checks, ticking, shirting and shaded fabrics. Reproduction fabrics of the Civil War Era 1840-1860 work well with this project.

General Supplies for all Blocks

- 1 ½ yards dark woven fabric for octagon block borders
- ¾ yards muslin for octagon template
- ¾ yard for setting triangles

- ⅛″ black poly ribbon or velvet ribbon
- ¼″ black poly ribbon or velvet ribbon
- ⅜″ black ribbed poly ribbon
- 1 black or brown pigma pen - fine point
- 1 black or brown pigma brush pen
- Black embroidery floss and needle
- 1″ clover bias maker

Step 1

OCTAGON TEMPLATE FOR CUTTING OUT BLOCKS

- Using the ¼ octagon pattern, trace onto a sheet of template plastic. See page 12 for template.
- Draw around pattern and cut out a ¼ octagon for a firm template.

- Cut a 23″ x 23″ square of muslin. Press out all wrinkles. Fold in half and half again. Press the fold lines.

- Lay plastic template over folded lines of muslin and draw around it. Cut on the pencil lines – you will have a 21″ x 21″ octagon.

- Use this muslin pattern template to lay over your background fabric that has been cut into a 23″ x 23″ square. Pin in place.

- Draw around muslin template and add a ¼″ seam allowance as you cut. Your block will be 21 ½″ x 21 ½″ – 21″ finished.

- Use the muslin template of the octagon shape for blocks #4, 5, & 9, which have a one-fabric background.

- Blocks #1, 2, 3, 6, 7, 8 have pieced backgrounds such as wallpaper and flooring or tables and sky, ground and a road. Individual block directions specify the measurements needed for the background pieces. Also if the background has stripes, you can line up the stripes in a straight line. These backgrounds need to be sewn together first, then using your octagon template, place the template over the pieced background fabric and draw around the octagon template and add a ¼″ seam allowance as you cut, referring to each picture of each block for placement.

Step 2

BORDERS AROUND EACH BLOCK

I suggest you use a woven plaid or check for the borders around each block to frame the images in the blocks. By sewing the strips around the blocks first, it allows you to place appliqués outside of the block using the borders as part of the picture.

- You can get 3 - 2″ x 12″ strips from 1 cut of 2″ x 36″ strip of woven fabric.

- You need 72 - 2″ x 12″ strips for the 9 blocks. Finished width of block borders is 1 ½″

- Cut 2″ strips, (this includes seam allowance) from selvedge to selvedge with your rotary cutter. Cut strips into 12″ lengths. Each block has 8 sides.

- Sew one strip at a time in a clockwise direction, crossing over the previous sewn strip. Trim the ends off of strips after all are sewn around the block. *See Figure 1.*

- Now you are ready to appliqué. Each block has individual directions for the trim on dresses, sleeves, faces, & quilts.

Step 3

APPLIQUÉS FOR EACH BLOCK

Each block has individual directions for appliqués.

- Add ¼″ seam allowance to all pattern pieces.

- Cut out all appliqué pieces for the block you are working on.

- Ink or embroider details on appliqués.

- Prepare all appliqués for hand or machine sewing.

FIG. 1

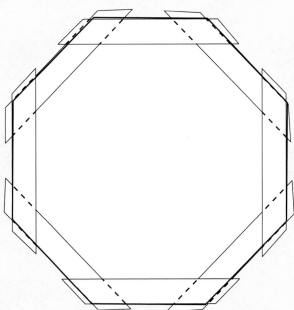

"Louisa supports the Alcott family with her Stories"

When I decided to make a "story" quilt featuring "cameo scenes" of Louisa's life and writing career, I designed the first block to reflect her love of writing. The image of a woman's hands holding a pen in her right hand came to mind. The hands needed sleeves, which provided an opportunity to show civil war era dress fabrics and style. Small paisleys printed on a fabric called "delaine", was the fabric of choice for women. Made of cotton and wool, delaine fabric was cool in the summertime and warm in the wintertime. The sleeves are made of a cotton reproduction of the historic delaine fabric. Louisa's writing desk, inkwell and pen frame the book that continues to be adored, "Little Women."

Louisa showed an interest and talent for writing early in her childhood. Her father was an intellectual and philosopher and maintained an extensive library. He created his own school, taught at a few local schools and gave lectures. He never came home with much money to support the family, but his influence on Louisa was great. Louisa had a free spirit and mind to think and reason for herself. This independent attitude and the parental encouragement led her to a writing career that supported the family.

One cold morning Louisa and her sisters found in the garden a little half-starved bird; and having warmed and fed it, Louisa was inspired to write a pretty poem to "The Robin." The fond mother was so delighted that she said to her, "You will grow up a Shakespeare!" This is the first recorded instance of her attempting to express her feelings in verse.[1]

– *Ednah D. Cheney*

TO THE FIRST ROBIN

Welcome, welcome, little stranger,
Fear no harm, and fear no danger;
We are glad to see you here,
For you sing "Sweet Spring is near."

Now the white snow melts away;
Now the flowers blossom gay:
Come dear bird and build your nest,
For we love our robin best.

Louisa May Alcott. Concord.
(written at eight years of age)

BLOCK ONE
"Louisa supports the Alcott family with her Stories"

Yardage

BACKGROUND

- Wallpaper - 11 ¼" x 23" floral stripe
- Writing desk – 12 ¼" x 23" wood grain or moiré-patterned fabric

APPLIQUÉS

- Sleeves 2 – 6" x 10" brown paisley
- Cuffs 2 – 3" x 3" contrasting small plaid
- Hands 2 – 4" x 5" flesh tone
- Pen and ink well 4" x 6" solid black
- Inkwell top 2" x 2" red
- Flower vase 4" x 5" shaded blue print
- Green stems 2 – 1" x 11" finished bias
- Flowers 3 – 4" x 4" of yellow print
- Sheet of paper 8 ½" x 11" ecru muslin
- For lettering "Little Women" – "Louisa May Alcott", embroidery floss & needle in brown or black, or use a brown or black pigma pen. The scroll background is optional.

Sewing Directions

Add ¼" seam allowance to all appliqué patterns.

- Sew wallpaper and desk fabrics together for the background block. Press seam.
- Referring to the General Directions, cut out octagon background block.
- Sew border strips around octagon.
- For the sleeves, cut 2 paisley rectangles 6" x 10" each – Turn under ¼" on each long side and baste. *See Figure 1.*
- Gather 1 end of each sleeve to 3". *See Figure 2.*
- For the cuffs, cut 2 plaid squares, 3" x 3". With right sides together sew 1 side of cuff to 3" gathered sleeve. Repeat for 2nd sleeve. *See Figure 3.*
- Fold cuff over seam and press. Turn cuff edges under ¼" and press. Fold in sides of cuff even with sleeve, press and baste all edges of the cuff. *See Figure 4.*

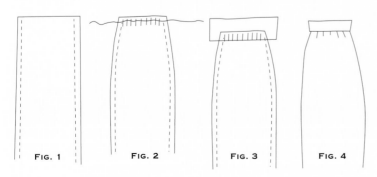

FIG. 1   FIG. 2   FIG. 3   FIG. 4

Sewing Directions

- For the stems, cut two 1″ x 11″ bias strips from your green fabric. Use your 1″ Clover bias maker to turn edges of strips to create the ½″ bias stems.

- Using the pigma pen trace or embroider (in an outline stitch) the fingers onto the hand fabric.

- Ink or embroider the 8 ½″ x 11″ rectangle page of "Little Women."

- Prepare all appliqués for hand or machine sewing.

- Sew the stopper in inkwell, the pen in the right hand and hands to cuffs of sleeves.

- Using the picture as a reference, place all objects on the pieced background, gluing or basting in place. Let ends of sleeves hang over border of block about 1 ½″ for right sleeve, and about 2″ for left sleeve. You will sew them down when blocks are assembled.

- Sew all pieces by hand or machine.

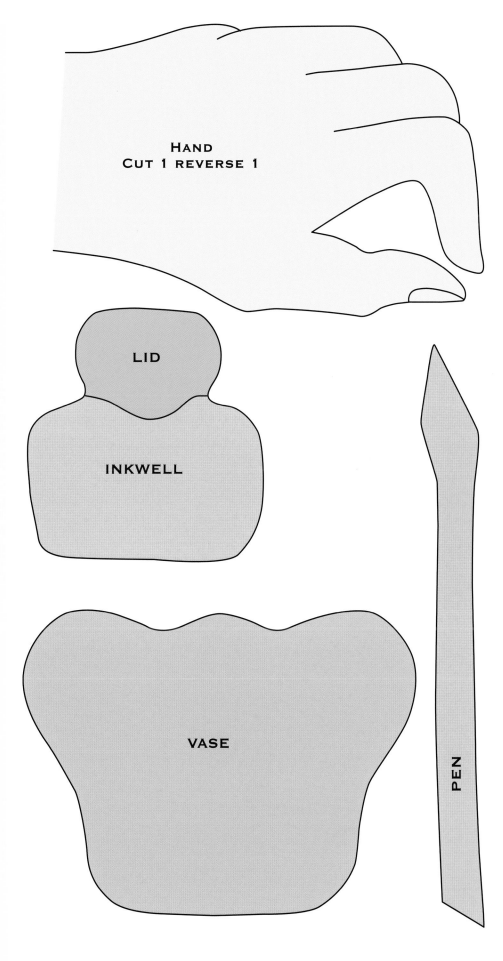

HAND
CUT 1 REVERSE 1

LID

INKWELL

VASE

PEN

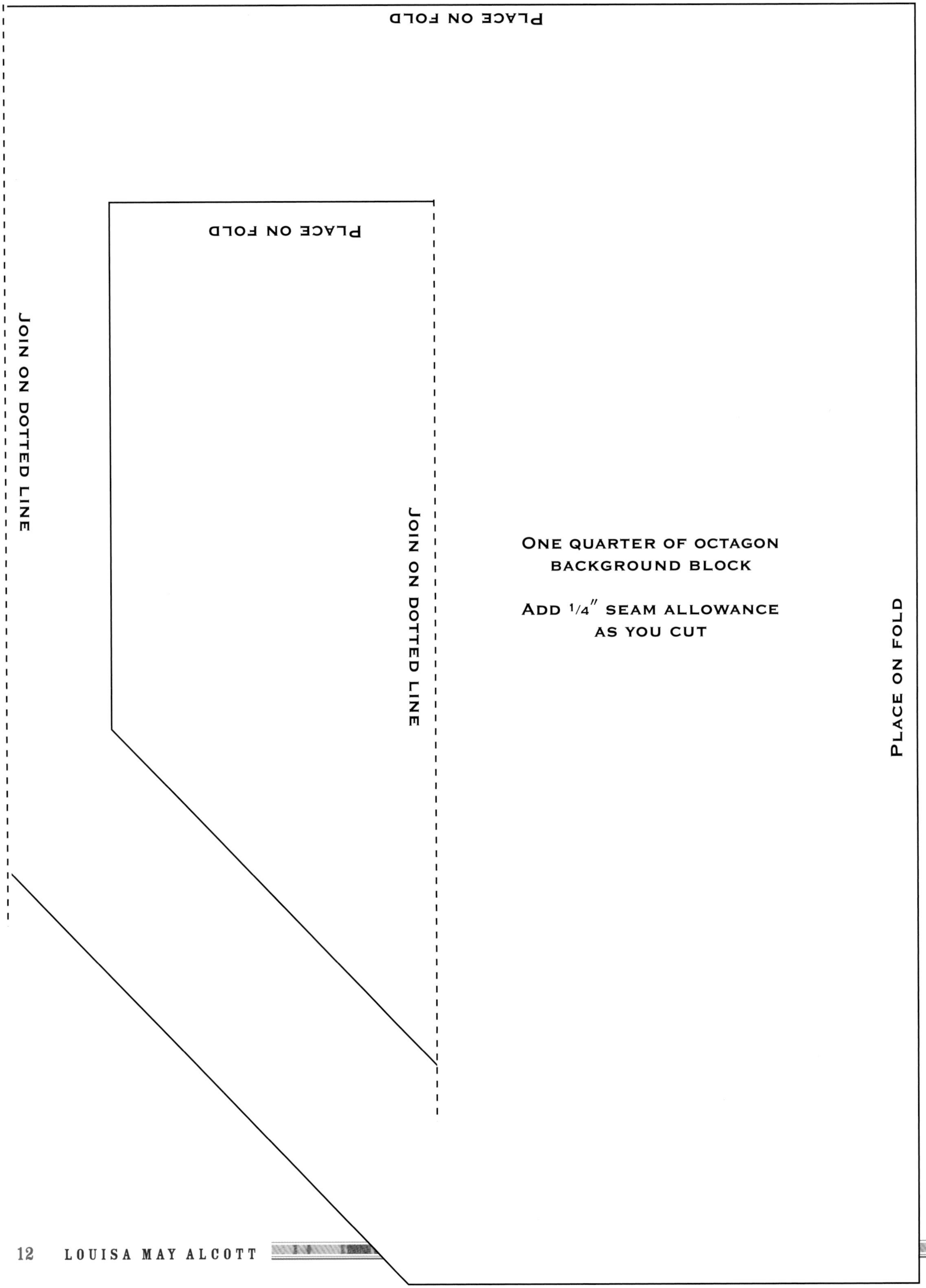

PLACE ON FOLD

PLACE ON FOLD

JOIN ON DOTTED LINE

JOIN ON DOTTED LINE

ONE QUARTER OF OCTAGON
BACKGROUND BLOCK

ADD ¼″ SEAM ALLOWANCE
AS YOU CUT

PLACE ON FOLD

PLACE ON FOLD

FLOWERS
Cut 3

LITTLE · WOMEN

LITTLE · WOMEN

LOUISA · M · ALCOTT

LOUISA · M · ALCOTT

"Abba, Louisa and Bronson attend a lecture by Clarina Nichols"

T his cameo scene of a women's rights lecture to shows the fashions c.1850-1865. When the Civil War broke out, men's Union uniforms were trimmed with military stripes on the coat sleeves and down the sides of their pants. Wives and children's clothing carried the same theme. Women sewed black velvet ribbons to the dress bodice, sleeves, and skirts. Abba's and Clarina's dresses show this style. The girl in the middle is young Louisa whose dress has an overskirt, and shorter sleeves. The white under sleeves were only worn by younger girls. Their full skirts were supported by narrow metal rings held together by twill tape, called "hoops" worn under the skirt. In 1850 the First Nations Women's Rights Convention was held in Worchester, Massachusetts only 37 miles from Concord. It is possible that the Alcotts took the train, as they often did, to Worchester to hear Clarina Nichol's lecture on women's rights.

A mos Bronson Alcott, the father of Louisa, was born Nov. 29, 1799. He derived his refined, gentle nature from his mother, who had faith in her son, and who lived to see him the accomplished scholar he had vowed to become in his boyhood. Although brought up in these rustic surroundings, his manners were always those of a true gentleman. Mrs. Alcott had a fine mind, and if she did not have large opportunities for scholastic instruction, she always enjoyed the benefit of intellectual society and converse with noble minds. She loved expression in writing, and her letters are full of wit and humor, keen criticism, and noble moral sentiments. It will be apparent from Louisa's life that she inherited the traits of both her parents, and that the uncommon powers of mind and heart that distinguished her were not accidental, but the accumulated result of the lives of generations of strong and noble men and women.[1]

– Ednah D.Cheney

March 1859 – *Busy life teaching, writing, sewing, getting all I can from lectures, books, and good people. Life is my college. May I graduate well, and earn some honors!*

– Louisa May Alcott

"Abba, Louisa and Bronson attend a lecture by Clarina Nichols"

Yardage

BACKGROUND

- Wallpaper – 19 ¼" x 23" of a striped ticking or print
- Floor - 4 ¼" x 23" of a tan moiré

APPLIQUÉS

DRESSES – to make plaid dresses more interesting, cut on the bias rather than straight on the plaid lines.

LOUISA MAY ALCOTT'S MOTHER Abba Alcott on the left is wearing a typical Civil War era style of dress. Women trimmed their sleeves, bodices and skirts with velvet ribbons appliquéd in an effort to emulate their men's military uniforms. This occurred even in children's clothes, boys and girls. Abba's black ribbon is a small ⅛" wide polyester ribbon found at fabric stores. The speaker at the women's rights lecture also trimmed her dress with the black ¼" ribbon.

- 1 roll each of black ¼" and ⅛" ribbon
- Green bench – 9 ½" x 16 ½" small green plaid or check
- Hands and heads for all figures – 5" x 5" flesh tone
- Abba's dress - 6 ½" x 7" red check or plaid
- Louisa's dress - 7 ½" x 8" purple plaid
- Shoes, hair, beard and belt – 3" x 4" black & brown
- Louisa's overskirt – 4" x 8" light purple print
- Louisa's undersleeves – 3" x 3" white
- Louisa's belt – 2" x 2" red check
- Bronson Alcott, her father, wears a suit of 8" x 8" small brown print with gold printed lapels, 3" x 4 ½"
- Bronson shirt – 1" x 2" ecru linen
- Lecture stage – 2 ½" x 9 ½" tan stripe
- Lecture fee basket – 2 ½" x 3 ½" yellow plaid

- Lecture hall banners – 3 ½" x 28 ½" shaded blue stripes
- Women's rights banner – 1 ½" x 4 ½" ecru linen
- Clarina Nichol's dress – 6" x 9" red print
- Banner pole – ¾" x 6" dark print

Sewing Directions

Add ¼" seam allowance to all appliqué patterns.

- Sew the floor fabric strip to the ticking wallpaper. Press seam.
- Referring to the General Directions cut out octagon background block.
- Sew border strips around octagon.
- Prepare all appliqués for hand or machine sewing.
- Ink the faces of all 3 people. Attach hair and beard.
- Cut out dresses for the 3 women.
- For Abba and Clarina, glue the ⅛" ribbon strips to the dress bodice, skirt and sleeves, tucking ends under garments. Attach head/neck and place hands

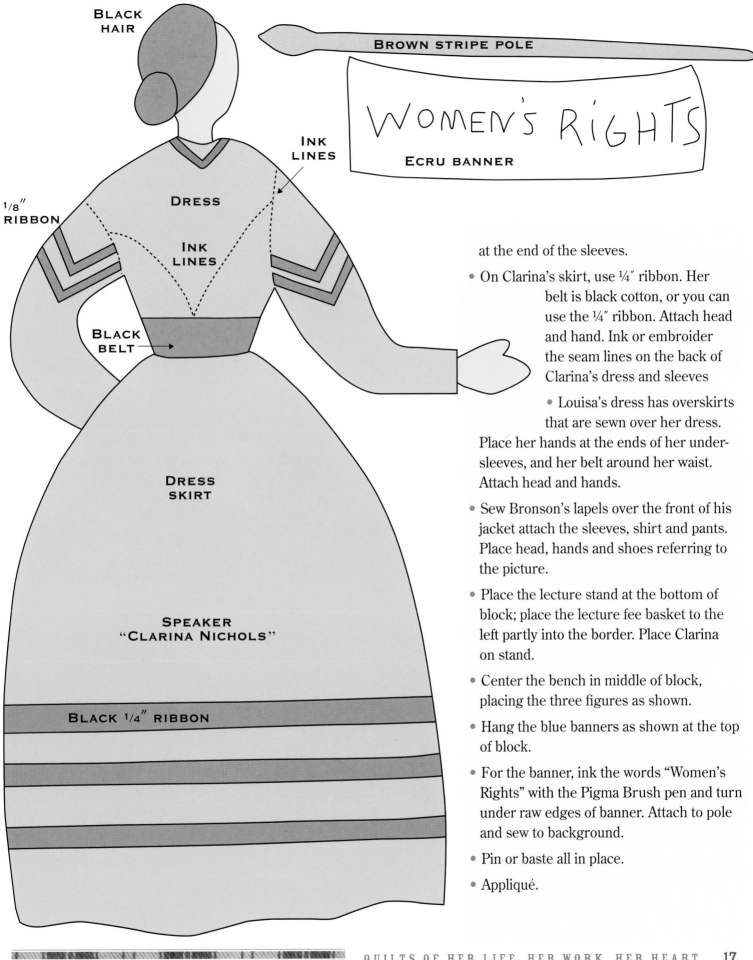

BLACK
HAIR

BROWN STRIPE POLE

INK
LINES

WOMEN'S RIGHTS

ECRU BANNER

DRESS

1/8″
RIBBON

INK
LINES

BLACK
BELT

DRESS
SKIRT

SPEAKER
"CLARINA NICHOLS"

BLACK 1/4″ RIBBON

at the end of the sleeves.

- On Clarina's skirt, use ¼″ ribbon. Her belt is black cotton, or you can use the ¼″ ribbon. Attach head and hand. Ink or embroider the seam lines on the back of Clarina's dress and sleeves

  - Louisa's dress has overskirts that are sewn over her dress. Place her hands at the ends of her under-sleeves, and her belt around her waist. Attach head and hands.

- Sew Bronson's lapels over the front of his jacket attach the sleeves, shirt and pants. Place head, hands and shoes referring to the picture.

- Place the lecture stand at the bottom of block; place the lecture fee basket to the left partly into the border. Place Clarina on stand.

- Center the bench in middle of block, placing the three figures as shown.

- Hang the blue banners as shown at the top of block.

- For the banner, ink the words "Women's Rights" with the Pigma Brush pen and turn under raw edges of banner. Attach to pole and sew to background.

- Pin or baste all in place.

- Appliqué.

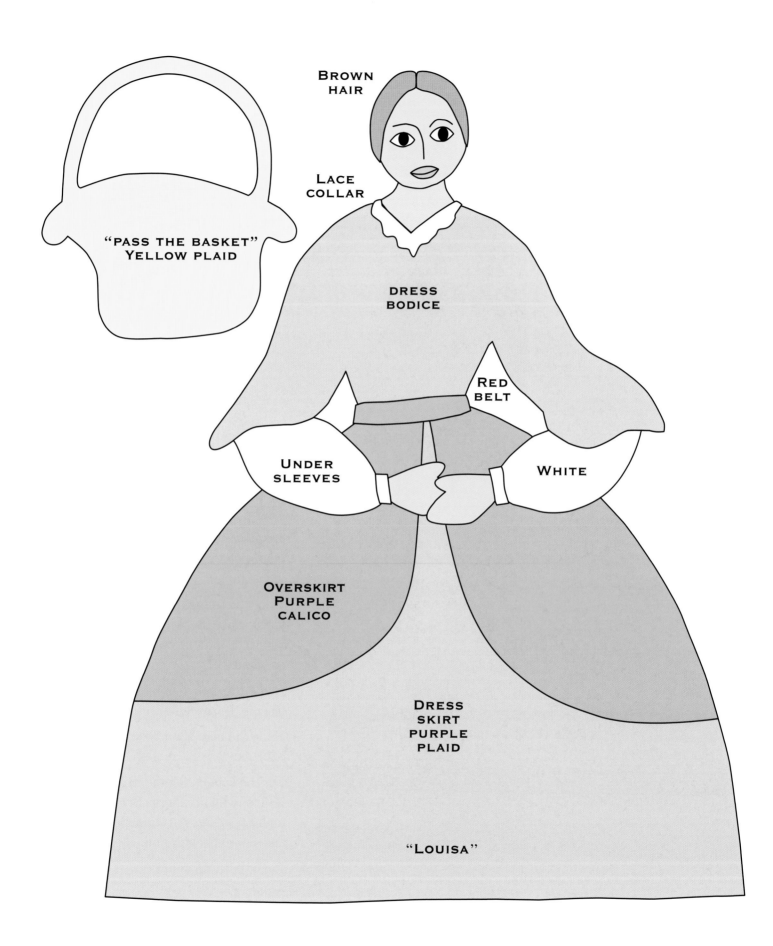

BROWN
HAIR

LACE
COLLAR

"PASS THE BASKET"
YELLOW PLAID

DRESS
BODICE

RED
BELT

UNDER
SLEEVES

WHITE

OVERSKIRT
PURPLE
CALICO

DRESS
SKIRT
PURPLE
PLAID

"LOUISA"

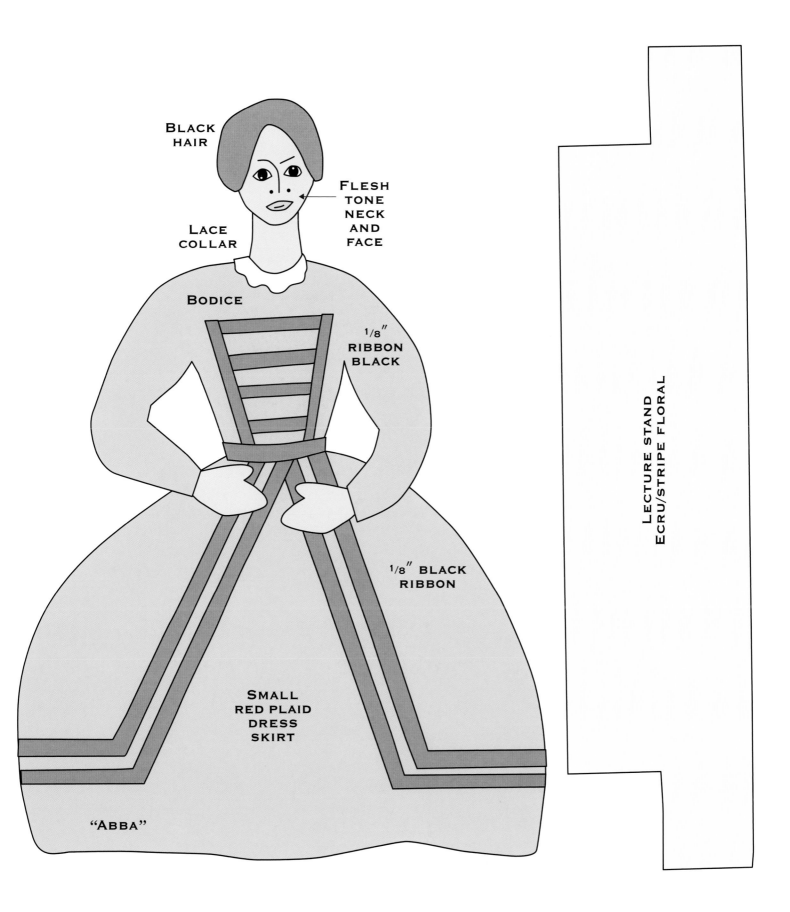

BLACK
HAIR

FLESH
TONE
NECK
AND
FACE

LACE
COLLAR

BODICE

1/8"
RIBBON
BLACK

1/8" BLACK
RIBBON

SMALL
RED PLAID
DRESS
SKIRT

"ABBA"

LECTURE STAND
ECRU/STRIPE FLORAL

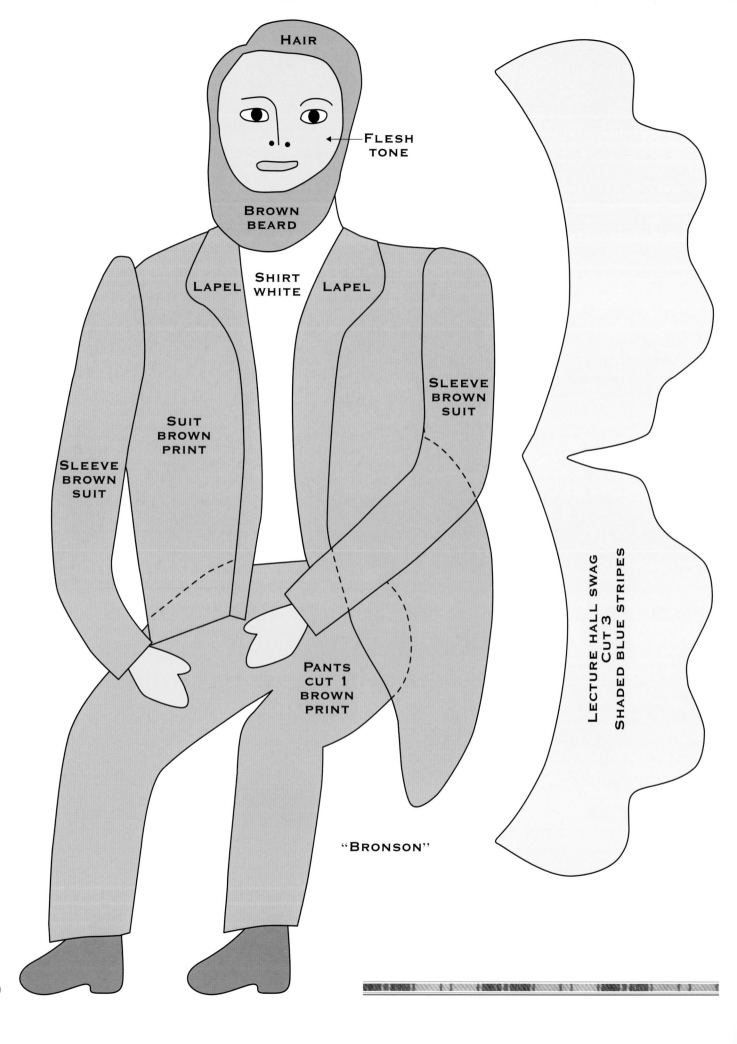

Hair

Flesh tone

Brown beard

Lapel Shirt white Lapel

Suit brown print

Sleeve brown suit

Sleeve brown suit

Pants cut 1 brown print

"Bronson"

Lecture hall swag
Cut 3
Shaded blue stripes

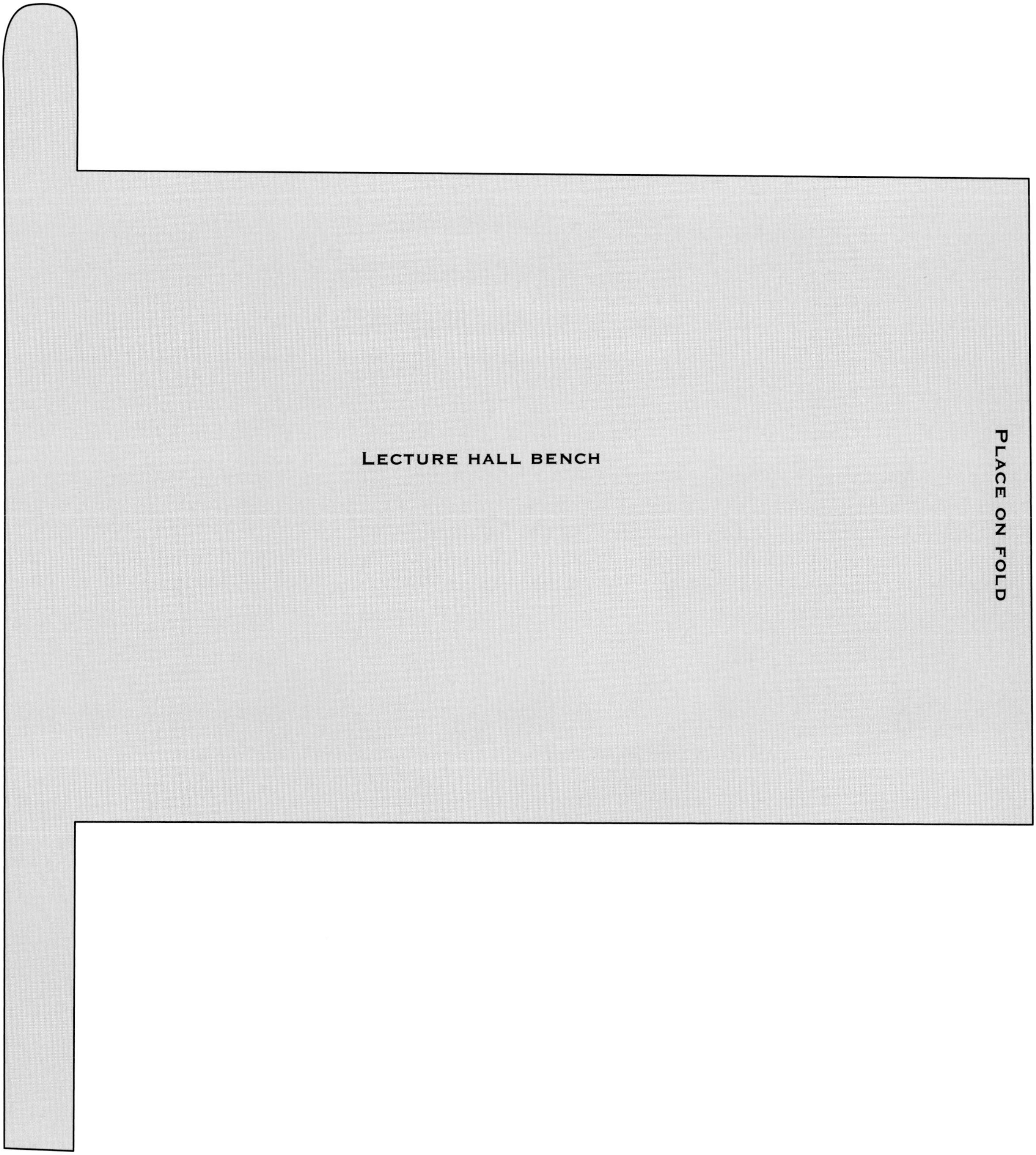

LECTURE HALL BENCH

PLACE ON FOLD

"First Woman to register to vote in her town of Concord, Mass."

This Civil War era tintype picture perfectly illustrates how a woman would dress if she were going to leave her home to shop, visit or vote. Her hair is neatly parted and pulled back into a bun. A small bonnet, drop earrings, mitts, a brooch and lace collar give an acceptable nod to the fashions of the era. But, what is a rarity in early pictures of women of this period is the beautiful paisley shawl wrapped around her shoulders, as if she is ready to step out of the door.

With the first & fourth corner blocks featuring Louisa's hands and sleeves, my editor, Kent Richards, suggested I carry that theme in all four corner blocks. This block captures an exciting moment for Louisa, a woman is allowed to vote. The plain calico sleeve trimmed with a black twill tape shows her support of the Union soldiers, and was a symbol of her abolitionist activism.

Ignited by the lectures and friends she made of the brave women who actively sought change, Louisa campaigned for the rights of women. She was the first woman in Concord to register to vote in a school election. Voters were required to show proof of taxes paid, which hers were not. She paid the tax bill and wrote in the Women's Journal, "I never did hanker to pay my taxes, but now am in a hurry to pay them."[2]

– Martha Saxton

"First Woman to register to vote in her town of Concord, Mass."

Yardage

BACKGROUND

- Wallpaper – 17 ¼″ x 23″ floral print
- Table – 6 ¼″ x 23″ blue stars print

APPLIQUÉS

- Voting box and lid – 8″ x 8″ red small check
- Curtains 2 - 11 ½″ x 11 ½″ blue plaid
- Ballot and vote sign – 3″ x 4 ½″ and 2″ x 4 ½″ creamy white
- Ballot box opening – 1 ½″ x 2″ black
- Hand – 4″ x 6″ flesh tone
- Flag canton 2 ½″ x 4″ blue star print
- Flag – white background – 4″ x 7 ½″
- Red strips on flag – 4″ x 7 ½″ – cut into (4) 1″ x 7 ½″ strips
- Sleeve – 6″ x 8 ½″ small floral, dark print
- Cuff – 2″ x 3 ½″ contrasting dress color
- Black braid trim – ³/₈″ wide x 18″ long for 2 strips
- Brown pigma pen for VOTE letters

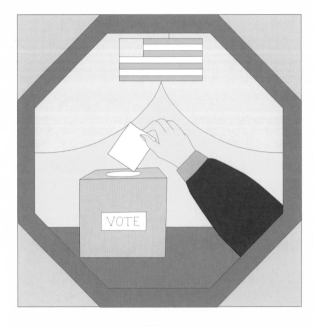

Sewing Directions

Add ¼″ seam allowance to all appliqué patterns.

- Sew the wallpaper and table fabrics together for the background block. Press seam.
- Referring to the General Directions cut out octagon background block.
- Sew border strips around octagon.
- Cut sleeve 6″ x 8 ½″, turn under ¼″ on each long side and baste. *See Figure 1.*
- Fold a pleat at the top of sleeve: fold corners under to make a 3″ sleeve end. Baste across top of sleeve to hold pleat and folds. *See Figure 2.*
- Cut one cuff. With right sides together sew 1 side of cuff to pleated sleeve. *See Figure 3.*
- Fold cuff over seam and press. Turn cuff edges under ¼″ and press. Fold in sides of cuff even with sleeve, press and baste all edges of the cuff. *See Figure 4.*
- Sew black braid on sleeve, taking a pleat at the top to turn.

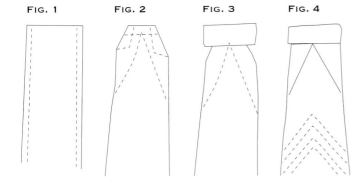

FIG. 1   FIG. 2   FIG. 3   FIG. 4

- Prepare all appliqués for hand or machine sewing.

- Appliqué box slit to box top. Baste box top to the top of ballot box. Sew in place.

- Ink or embroider VOTE on white rectangle. Sew to middle of ballot box.

- Using the pigma pen trace or embroider (in an outline stitch) the fingers onto the hand fabric.

- Place ballot inside thumb and first finger, then place the hand in sleeve, pin and baste to edge of the lower right border of the block.

- Place curtains in middle, top of block, overlapping at the top. Sew in place along edge of border strip around block.

- Sew other appliqués in place.

Flag

- Cut out white background – this serves as white stripes.

- Place canton in left hand corner of white background. Turn all edges under.

- Pin and sew in place.

- Place 4 red stripes on white background. Cut stripes to fit. Pin and baste. Sew in place.

- Pin flag in the center of curtains and sew in place.

BLUE STAR CANTON	**RED**	
	WHITE	
	RED	
WHITE		
RED		
WHITE		
RED		

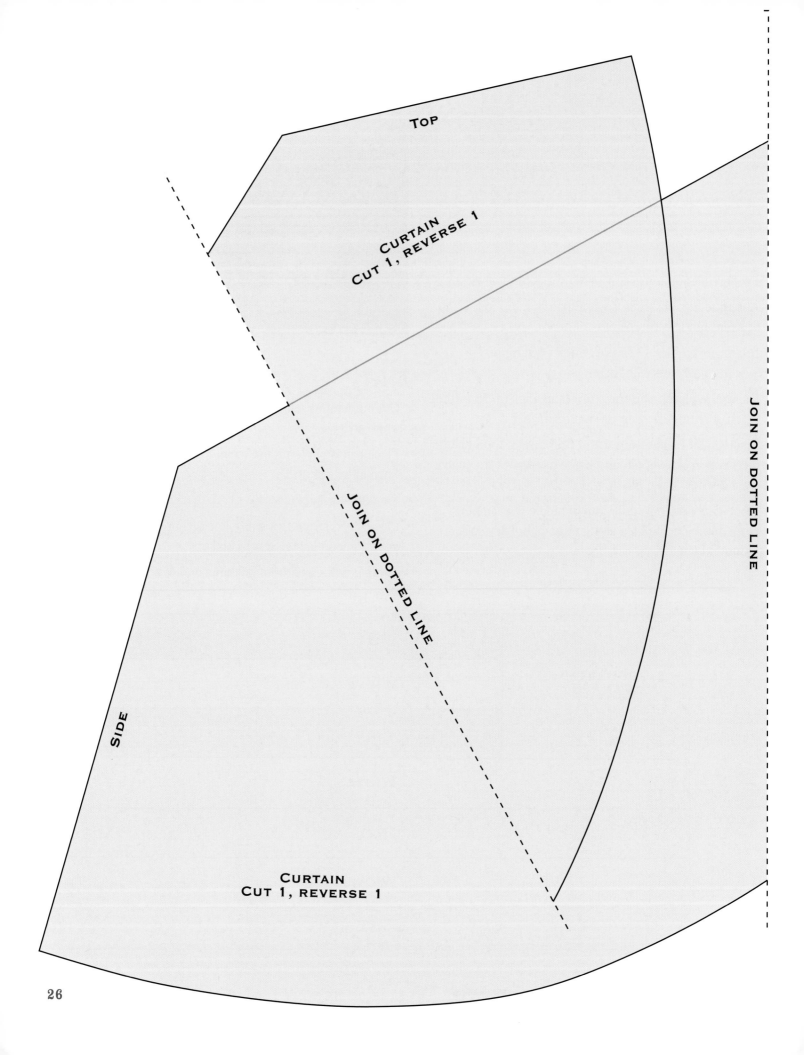

TOP

CURTAIN
CUT 1, REVERSE 1

JOIN ON DOTTED LINE

JOIN ON DOTTED LINE

SIDE

CURTAIN
CUT 1, REVERSE 1

26

BALLOT
CUT 1

HAND
CUT 1

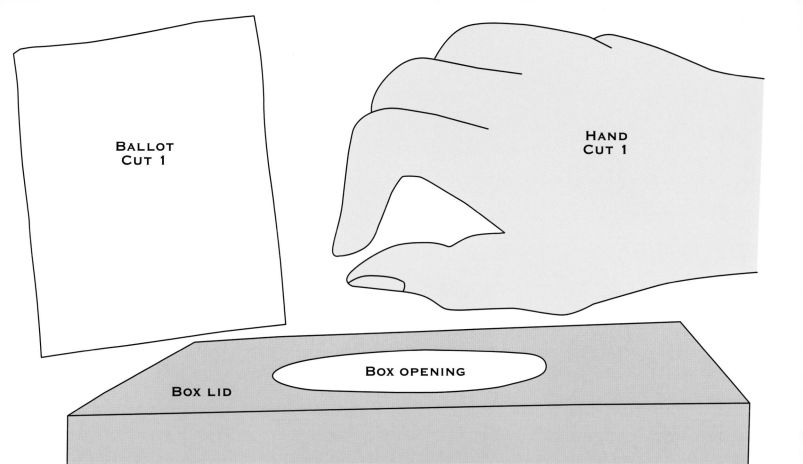

BOX OPENING

BOX LID

BALLOT BOX

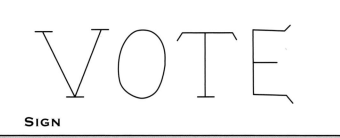

VOTE

SIGN

"Safe House?"

This block shows two Alcott sisters climbing a ladder to pick apples, sometimes their only food. The Alcotts suffered great poverty because Bronson earned little money. Poor as they were, the Alcotts' harbored runaway slaves and shared their meager food supply with the poor.

The escaped slave girl's dress and apron are made of homespun with a pink printed apron and cape. Her turban is made of ticking. The Alcott sister's dresses are made of madder dyed reproduction prints. Stripes and homespun checks were favorite fabrics for house wear. I found inspiration for this block in a cameo scene from "Godey's Lady's Book –1860."

"Safe House?" speaks to the risks taken by the runaway slaves and the families who sheltered them from slave catchers. The Alcotts strongly supported the anti-slavery cause. In this block the slave girl hides behind the spring house, hoping she can trust this family to hide and feed her and then help her to find the next safe house on the Underground Railroad.

From Godey's Ladies Book 1860

Yardage

BACKGROUND

- 1 - 23″ x 23″ light floral background print that recedes as a background and does not overwhelm the figures of the women.

APPLIQUÉS

SLAVE GIRL

- For dress – 4″ x 7″ small brown check
- Apron and cape – 4″ x 7″ small pink stripe print
- Face and hand – 2″ x 2″ dark brown solid
- Shoes – 2″ x 2″ black solid – also for Elizabeth on ladder
- Turban – 2″ x 2″ striped ticking

ALCOTT WOMEN

- Anna's dress – 6″ x 7″ dark red plaid
- Anna's overskirt – 4″ x 5″ – red check
- Anna's hair – 2″ x 2″ light brown
- Head, neck, hands for both girls – 4″ x 4″ flesh tone
- Elizabeth's apron – 4″ x 6″ yellow/gold strip woven
- Elizabeth's hair – 2 ½″ x 2 ½″ yellow dot
- Elizabeth's dress – 8″ x 8″ rusty red print
- Elizabeth's undersleeves – 2″ x 4″

SPRING HOUSE

- 5″ x 6″ organic red print
- Roof and door – 5″ x 8″ wood brown moiré
- Z boards on door – 1″ x 8″ black textured print

APPLE TREE ETC.

- 12″ x 12″ apple green leafy print

- Trunk and limbs – 9″ x 12″ moiré wood print
- Apples – for 8 apples – 2 ½″ x 18″ strip of red plaid also use plaid for rim of the basket
- Apple leaf – scrap of green
- Basket – 3 ½″ x 4″ of yellow plaid
- Water pitcher – 3″ x 4″ blue striped ticking
- Ladder – 6 ½″ x 12 ½″ dark brown moiré

Sewing Directions

Add ¼″ seam allowance to all appliqué patterns.

- Cut 23″ x 23″ background block out of 1 piece of a neutral fabric.
- Referring to the General Directions cut out octagon background block.
- Sew borders around background block.
- Cut 2 – 1 ½″ x 12 ½″ ladder poles.

- Cut 4 – 1″ x 2 ½″ rungs for ladders.

- Sew 3 rungs to poles at the bottom of the ladder about 1″ apart.

- Sew 1 rung about 2 ¾″ down from the top of the ladder poles.

- Prepare all appliqués for hand or machine appliqué.

- Embroider or ink face of Elizabeth.

- Referring to the picture, assemble the women with their heads, skirts, aprons, sleeves and hands. Sew the apples on the tree and the tree to the trunk. Sew the rungs on the ladders. Sew the door and roof to the Spring House.

- Pin all figures in place referring to the picture.

- Pin, baste and sew in place.

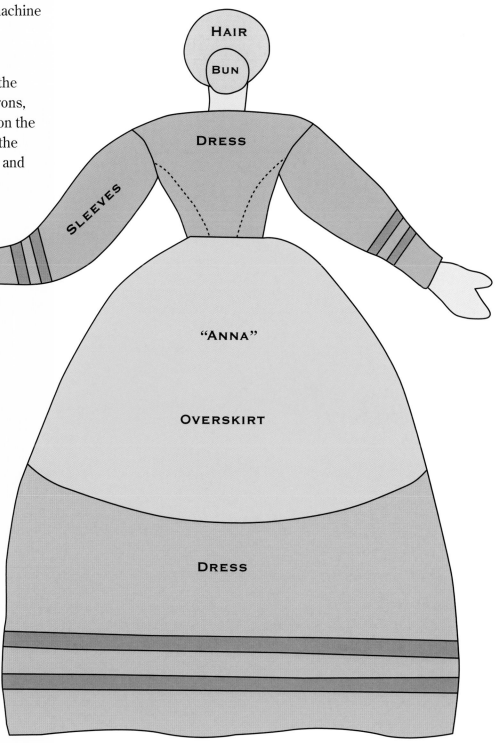

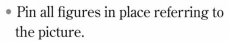

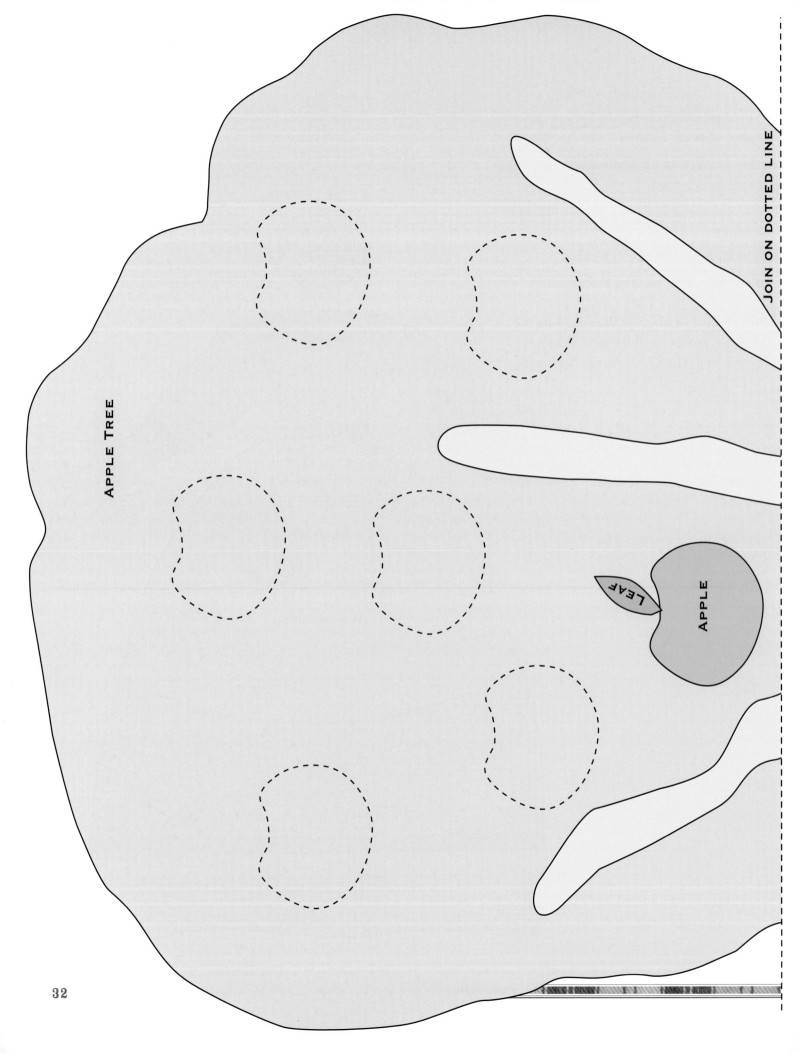

APPLE TREE

APPLE

LEAF

JOIN ON DOTTED LINE

32

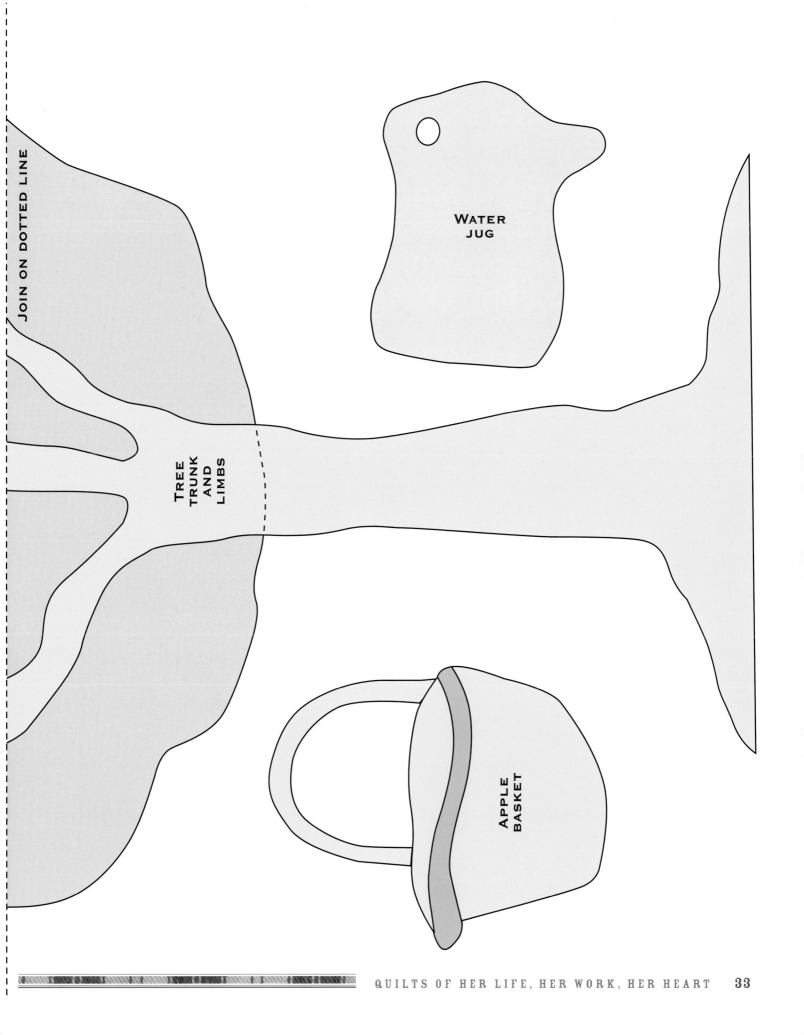

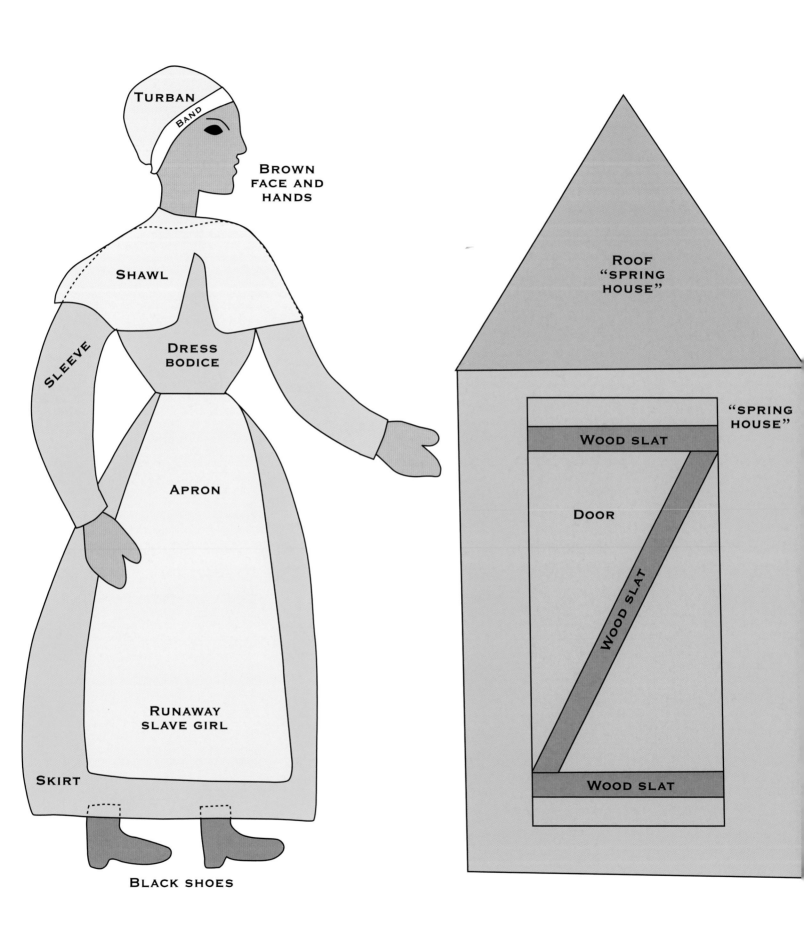

TURBAN

BAND

BROWN
FACE AND
HANDS

SHAWL

SLEEVE

DRESS
BODICE

APRON

RUNAWAY
SLAVE GIRL

SKIRT

BLACK SHOES

ROOF
"SPRING
HOUSE"

"SPRING
HOUSE"

WOOD SLAT

DOOR

WOOD SLAT

WOOD SLAT

HAIR

DRESS bodice

BIB

DRESS skirt

APRON

"Elizabeth"

BLACK SHOES

"Orchard House"

Orchard House was a safe haven for the Alcott family. Bronson's knowledge of carpentry restored the house and provided privacy for Louisa and her writing. She still took in sewing to provide for the Alcott family.

After Louisa achieved much success as an author, she lived in Boston, traveled to Europe and stayed with friends. She always came home to Orchard House where her family members came and went, always needing her help and advice. She sacrificed her plans time and time again to manage the flow of her fathers philosopher friends, who came to attend his seminars at Orchard House.

Mr. Alcott sought such work as he could find to do with his hands; but it was scanty and insufficient. Mrs. Alcott subdued her proud heart to the necessity of seeking help from friends. They had a few rooms in the house of a kind neighbor, who welcomed them to her house, in addition to her own large family; and there they struggled with the poverty which Louisa for the first time fully realized.

Yet her journal says little of the hardships they endured, but is full of her mental and moral struggles. It was characteristic of this family that they never were conquered by their surroundings. Mr. Alcott might retire into sad and silent musing, Mrs. Alcott's warm, quick temper, might burst out into flame, the children might be quarrelsome or noisy; but their ideal of life always remained high, fresh, and ennobling. Their souls always "knew their destiny divine," and believed that they would find fitting expression in life some time.[1]

- Ednah D. Cheney

BLOCK FIVE "Orchard House"

Yardage

BACKGROUND

- 1 - 23″ x 23″ floral medium dark "purplish″ print

APPLIQUÉS

- House – 9″ x 12″ red/yellow woven plaid
- Windows – 9″ x 12″ yellow plaid, cut so there is a light center and darker top and bottom eaves
- Door – 3″ x 4″ rusty red floral print
- Chimney – 3″ x 4″ rusty red floral print (same as door)
- Porch and posts – 3″ x 7″ brown/purple print
- Porch roof – 3″ x 6″ red check woven
- Roof peak – 6″ x 10″ red check woven
- House roof – 4″x 18″ brown/purple print
- Trees – 6″ x 16″ organic greens
- Purple flowers – 2 ½″ x 12″ strip of purple print – 2″ x 2″ yellow for flower centers
- Yellow flowers – 4″ x 9″ strip of yellow print
- Green flower stems – 1″ x 12″ bias strip

Sewing Directions

Add a ¼″ seam allowance to all appliqué templates.

- Cut 23″ x 23″ background block out of 1 piece of background fabric.
- Referring to the General Directions cut out octagon background block.
- Sew borders around background block.
- Prepare all appliqués for hand or machine appliqué.

- Use the picture as a guide. Lay out all cut pieces of the house. Start with the house and windows, then door, posts and porch step.
- Next assemble parts for roof, peak and chimney. Baste to top of house.
- Pin and baste house units together.
- Center house in middle of block. Place trees underneath the roof and chimney, pin and baste. Pin and baste house.
- For the stems, cut one 1″ x 12″ bias strip from your green fabric. Use your 1″ Clover bias maker to turn edges of strips to create the ½″ bias stems. Cut in half for two stems. Pin and baste stems and all flowers.
- Sew all pieces by hand or machine.

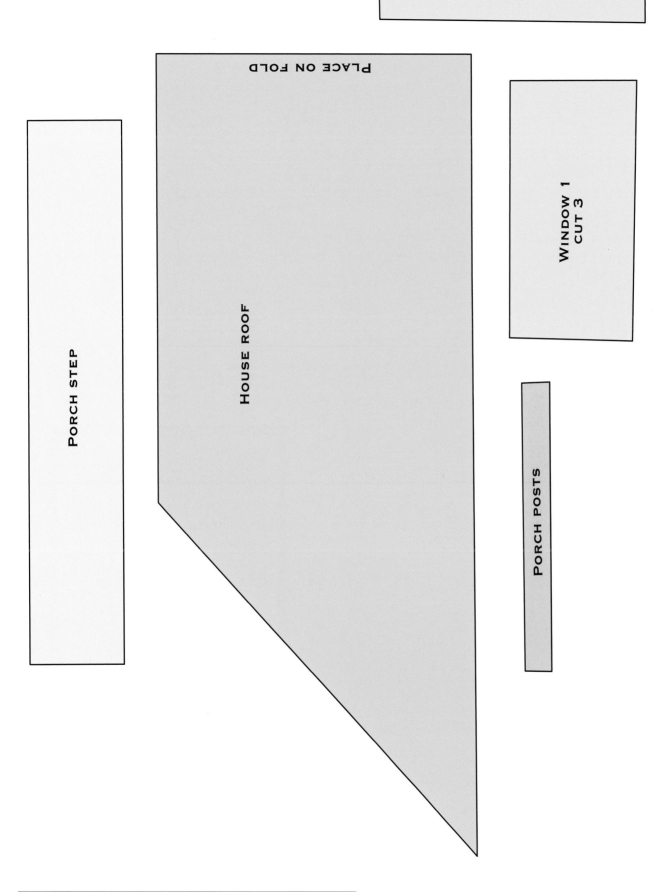

WINDOW 2
CUT 4

WINDOW 1
CUT 3

PLACE ON FOLD

HOUSE ROOF

PORCH STEP

PORCH POSTS

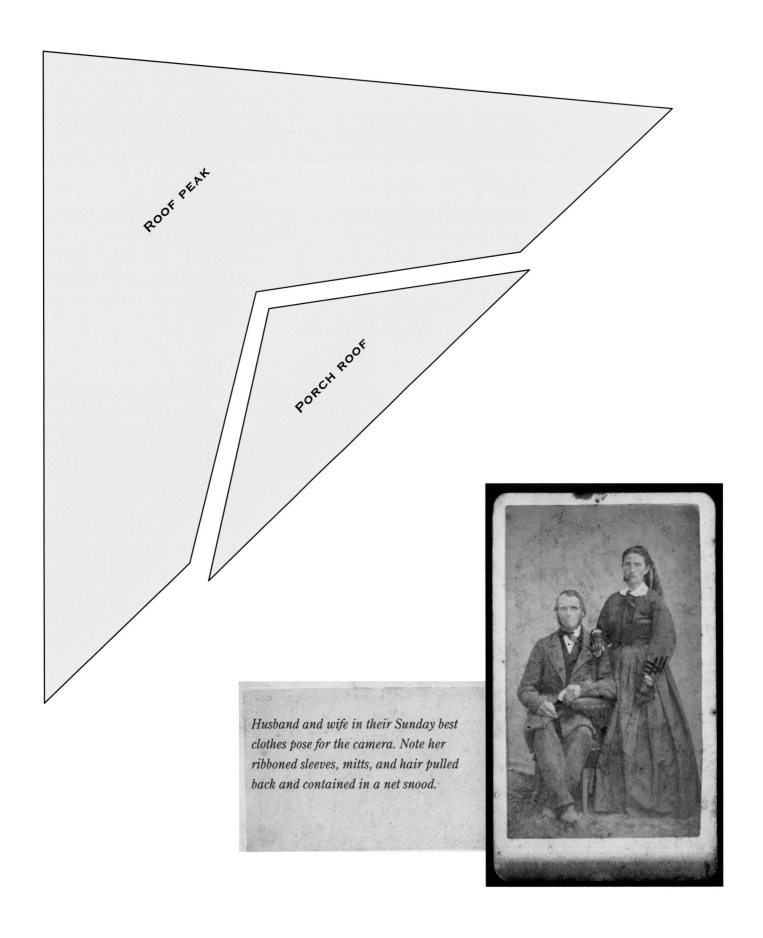

ROOF PEAK

PORCH ROOF

Husband and wife in their Sunday best
clothes pose for the camera. Note her
ribboned sleeves, mitts, and hair pulled
back and contained in a net snood.

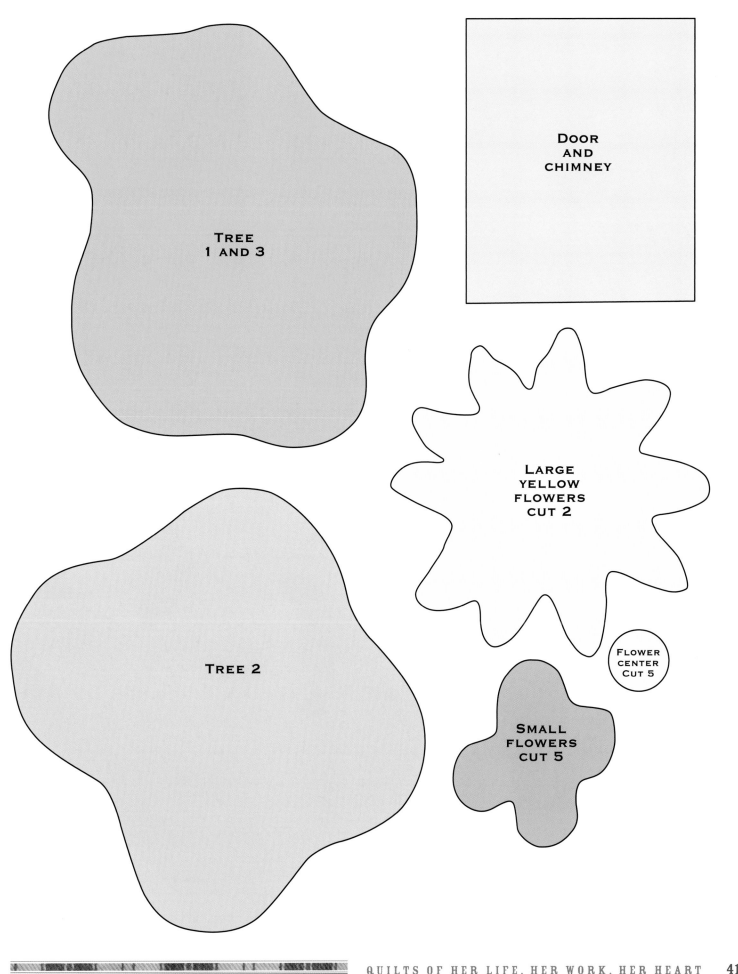

TREE
1 AND 3

DOOR
AND
CHIMNEY

LARGE
YELLOW
FLOWERS
CUT 2

FLOWER
CENTER
CUT 5

TREE 2

SMALL
FLOWERS
CUT 5

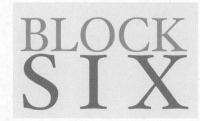
"Keep your eyes on the North Star and watch out for Slave Catchers"

I chose shaded blue, brown and green for the sky and grounds. I wanted the focus of the Cameo to be nightfall, when it would be the safest time to escape. The runaway slave woman wears woven ticking for her dress and a turban. The hay bale in the wagon provides protection for her child, as he watches out the back as they follow the North Star to their freedom in Canada.

Antislavery groups formed a network of safe houses that provided shelter, food and safe passage for runaway slaves or "contraband". Louisa notes in her journal, "Mother hid a contraband in the oven." Sometimes slaves were given nice clothing so they could travel north, out in the open in the daytime. This woman and her son chose to travel at night, ever watchful for slave catchers.

I became an abolitionist at a very early age, but have never been able to decide whether I was made so by seeing the portrait of George Thompson hidden under a bed in our house during the Garrison riot, and going to comfort "the poor man who had been good to the slaves," or because I was saved from drowning in the frog pond some years later by a colored boy. However that may be, the conversion was genuine; and my greatest pride is in the fact that I lived to know the brave women and men who did so much for the cause, and that I had a very small share in the war which put an end to a great wrong.

– Louisa May Alcott

Yardage

BACKGROUND

- Background block - three strips of fabric; night blue sky, tan or brown road, and green for grass.
- Sky - 12″ x 23″ shaded blue night sky
- Road - 6″ x 23″ shaded brown or tan
- Grass - 12″ x 23″ shaded green

APPLIQUÉS

- Trees – 4 - 5″ x 6″ strip of green, or 4 different greens
- Tree trunks – 4 - 3″ x 16″ strip of dark brown
- Clouds – 2 - 4″ x 13″ strip of gray blue
- North Star – 7″ x 7″ square of gold print
- Horse – 8″ x 8″ square of red/brown
- Horse collar, tail, mane – 3″ x 5″ strip of black
- Wagon, wheels, hitch pole, wheel centers – 8″ x 12″ strip of light brown moiré print
- Slave woman's head, hand, foot and son's head – 3″ x 3″ dark brown
- Boys straw hat – 2″ x 2″ yellow gold
- Hay bale and cape trim – 4 ½″ x 4 ½″ gold/brown check
- Dress and turban – 4″ x 5 ½″ striped ticking
- Cape – 3″ x 3″ red plaid
- Wheel spokes – 17″ of ¼″ poly ribbon
- Bridle and reins – 15″ of ⅛″ ribbon
- Pigma pen for shadowing over wheels of wagon and horses eye.

Sewing Directions

Add ¼″ seam allowance to all appliqué patterns.

- Assemble the road template and cut out road.
- Lay out the 3 background strips of sky, road, and grass. Sew together as seen in picture. Press seams. Cut sewn block down to 23″ x 23″.

- Referring to the General Directions cut out octagon background block.
- Sew border strips around octagon.
- Prepare all appliqués for hand or machine sewing.

WAGON – Cut out wagon wheels and centers, wagon and poles – Lay out 8 strips of ¼″ ribbon for spokes and glue to inside rim of wheel. Place center of wheel over ribbons where they cross. Sew wheels to wagon.

HORSE – Make a bridle out of ⅛″ ribbon and glue to horse's head. Sew mane, harness and tail. Ink a dot for the horse's eye as shown.

SLAVE WOMAN – Cut out cape and trim. Sew trim to cape, turban to her head, and hand to sleeve. Place cape on her back and sew all pieces to dress including her bare foot.

- Pin all in place on background.
- Place poles on wagon and horse as shown.
- Place hay bale and little boy inside wagon, woman on the wagon seat.
- Place a ⅛″ x 8 ½″ ribbon from her hand to the horses' bridle, let the end of ribbon dangle from her hand.
- Pin trees, trunks, star and clouds according to the picture.
- Baste all appliqués.
- Sew all pieces by hand or machine.

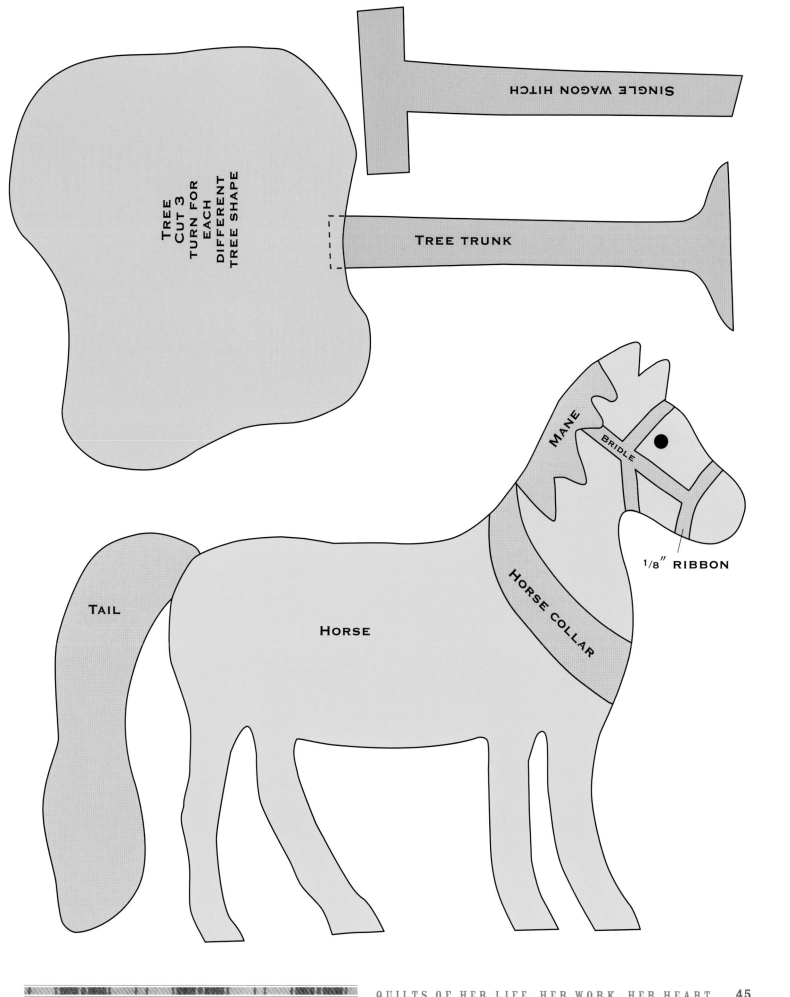

TREE
CUT 3
TURN FOR
EACH
DIFFERENT
TREE SHAPE

SINGLE WAGON HITCH

TREE TRUNK

MANE

BRIDLE

¹/8″ RIBBON

TAIL

HORSE

HORSE COLLAR

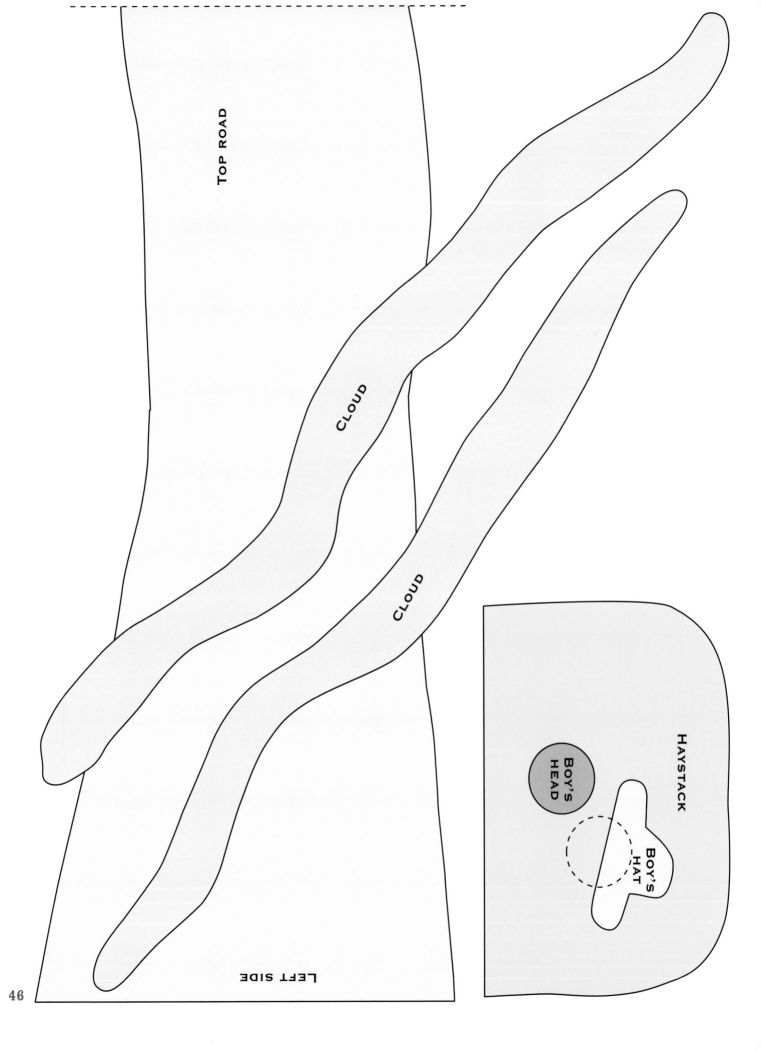

TOP ROAD

CLOUD

CLOUD

LEFT SIDE

HAYSTACK

BOY'S HEAD

BOY'S HAT

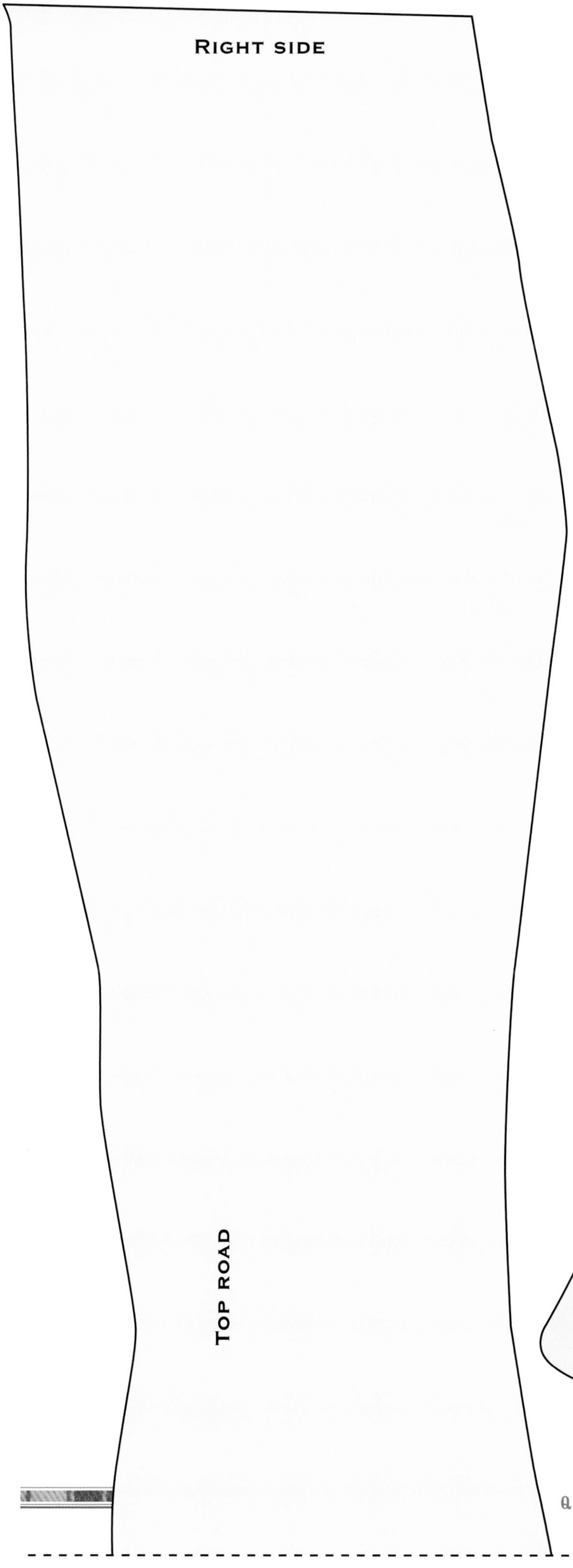

RIGHT SIDE

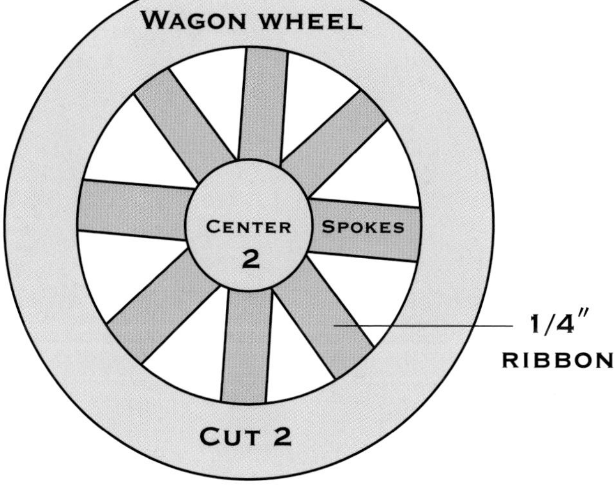

WAGON WHEEL

CENTER
2

SPOKES

1/4"
RIBBON

CUT 2

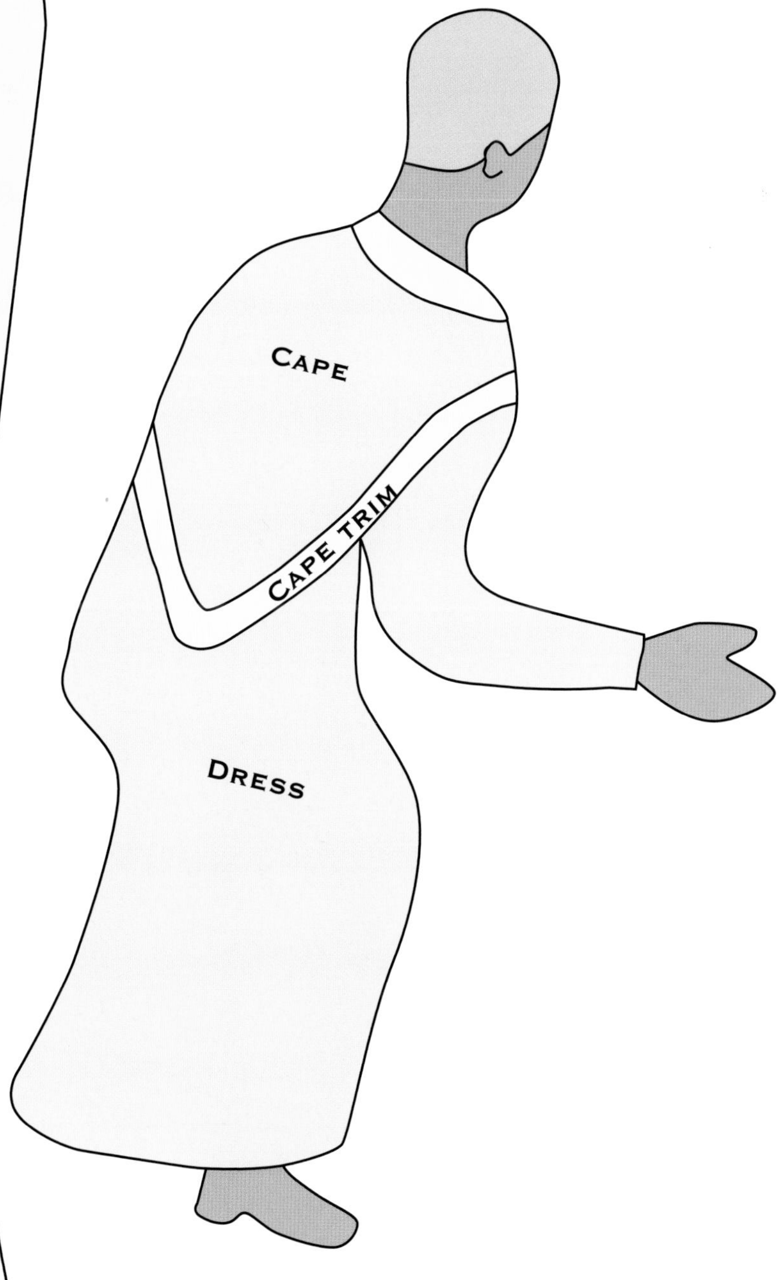

TOP ROAD

CAPE

CAPE TRIM

DRESS

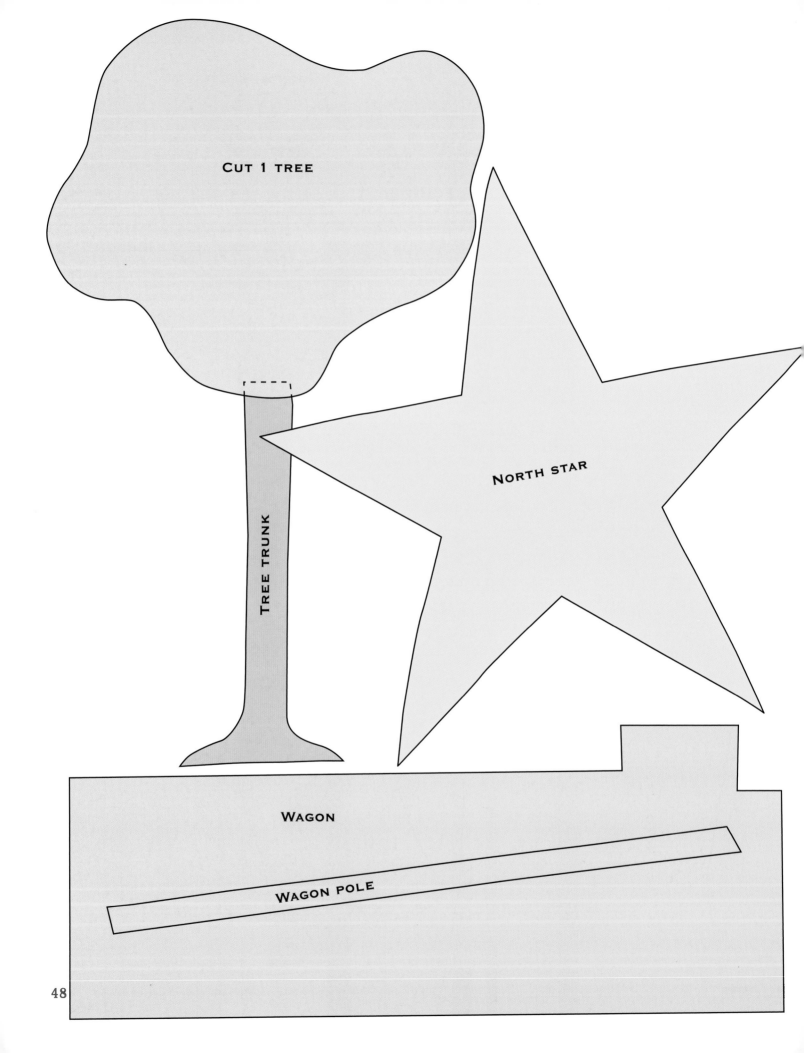

Cut 1 tree

Tree trunk

North star

Wagon

Wagon pole

48

Dressing the Women

I enjoyed "dressing" the women in the blocks. Using vintage Civil War era photographs as a reference, I learned that certain dress, hair, and jewelry styles were consistent among older women, younger women and girls.

Skirts were supported by round steel rings, held together by twill tape and tied around the waist. Belts with large buckles emphasized small waistlines. Small crocheted white collars graced the neck of the dress, secured by a brooch. The collar protected the neck of the dress from body oils.

Hair was parted in the middle and pulled to the back of the head in a bun and secured with a large comb. Women also wore "sausage curls" that hung in ringlets on each side of her face. Long, drop earrings hung from the ears as net mitts covered the hands.

Younger women adopted a fashionable look of their own. Sleeves were elbow length and required an "under sleeve" to cover the rest of the arm. Little girls from babyhood to about twelve or fourteen years of age wore "off the shoulder" necklines and small earrings.

Many of the dresses women wore during the Civil War time period were made of delaine, a wool and cotton fabric. Piping was placed in the seams of the sleeve armholes, around the bottom of the bodice to add strength to sewn seams. Dropped shoulder seams and a "V" shaped back bodice were common.

During the war years dressmakers placed black velvet ribbons on the bodice, sleeves and skirt to imitate the military look of soldier's uniforms. Women fought their own war by keeping the home front going while their men went to fight the War Between the States.

"Making Quilts for Soldiers"

Wives, mothers, sisters of Union soldiers made their needles and thread "fly" as they quickly sewed up quilts and comforts for their fighting men and boys. Sewing groups set aside sewing their own quilts and sent thousands of long, narrow quilts to the Sanitary Commission in Boston to be distributed to the troops. On the table I placed a needle case, spool of thread, thimble, a pocket, a make do pincushion, all tools for making quilts and shirts for Union men and boys.

1861 April. – *War declared with the South, and our Concord company went to Washington. A busy time getting them ready, and a sad day seeing them off; for in a little town like this we all seem like one family in times like these. At the station the scene was very dramatic, as the brave boys went away perhaps never to come back again.*

I've often longed to see a war, and now I have my wish. I long to be a man; but as I can't fight, I will content myself with working for those who can.

Stories simmered in my brain, demanding to be writ; but I let them simmer, knowing that the longer the divine afflatus was bottled up the better it would be.

1861 May. – *Spent our May-day working for our men, - three hundred women all sewing together at the hall for two days.*

1861 October. – *All together on Marmee's birthday. Sewing and knitting for "our boys" all the time. It seems as if a few energetic women could carry on the war better than the men do it so far.*

– Louisa May Alcott

Yardage

BACKGROUND

- Wallpaper – 10″ x 23″ strip of a light floral print
- Sewing table – 13″ x 23″ piece of plaid or print that will contrast the sewing tools on the table

APPLIQUÉS

- Sleeves - 2 - 6 ¼″ x 10 ½″ dark red or cinnamon brown cotton print
- Cuffs - 2 - 3″ x 3″ square contrasting to the sleeves
- Hands - 2 - 4″ x 5″ flesh tone
- Sewing basket and handle - 5 ½″ x 7″ of a medium red print
- Thread spool - 2 ½″ x 3 ½″ red check. Wrap a yellow or gold perle cotton thread around spool
- Needle case - 2″ x 3 ½″ rectangle of a red plaid and a 1 ½″ length of ⅛″ wide black ribbon
- Pocket - 4 ½″ x 4 ½″ square of a yellow print and a 2 ½″ x 1″ ticking for lining
- Make Do Strawberry Pincushion - 3 ½″ x 4″ small pink print for strawberries, and a 2″ x 4″ rectangle of green plaid or dot for the 3 leaves at the bottom of strawberry
- Candleholder stand - 3 ½″ x 4 ½″ rectangle of a tiny gold dot or print
- Thimble 3″ x 3″ brown calico
- Scissors 3″ x 5″ gold solid

MINIATURE "FLYING GEESE" SOLDIERS QUILT:

- Scraps of red, blue, green, gold, and rust for Flying Geese
- Scraps of neutrals for the backgrounds
- ¼ yard brown for border

Sewing Directions

Add ¼″ seam allowance to all appliqué patterns.

- Sew wallpaper and desk fabrics together for the background block. Press seam.
- Referring to the General Directions cut out octagon background block.
- Sew border strips around octagon.
- Prepare all appliqués for hand or machine sewing.
- For the sleeves, cut 2 rectangles 6 ¼″ x 10 ½″ each – Turn under ¼″ on each long side and baste. *See Figure 1.*
- Gather 1 end of each sleeve to 3″. *See Figure 2.*
- For the cuffs, cut squares, 3″ x 3″. With right sides together sew 1 side of cuff to 3″ gathered sleeve. Repeat for 2nd sleeve. *See Figure 3.*
- Fold cuff over seam and press. Turn cuff edges under ¼″ and press. Fold in sides of cuff even with sleeve, press and baste all edges of the cuff. *See Figure 4.*

- Using the pigma pen trace or embroider (in an outline stitch) the fingers onto the hand fabric.

- Place the right thumb and forefinger into the handles of the scissors.

ASSEMBLE THE FLYING GEESE QUILT:

13″ x 15 ½″ finished

- Cut 27 light and 27 dark 2 ⅜″ squares. Cut each on the diagonal for 54 light and 54 dark triangles. *See Figure 5.*

FIG. 5

- Piece 1 light and 1 dark triangle to create a square. (You need to make 2 of each light/dark square so that when you sew them together they form a Flying Geese out of the same fabrics.) Squares will be 1 ½″ finished.

- Match the two same squares and sew together with dark side matching to create the geese.

- Create three rows of 9 flying geese. *See Figure 6.*

- Cut 4 strips 1 ½″ x 14″ to set on each side of the flying geese blocks.

- Cut 2 strips 1 ½″ x 13 ½″ for the top and bottom border. Sew geese and strips together. Add top and bottom border. *See Figure 7.*

- Referring to the picture, place the quilt on the background and the hands on top of it. Pin in place.

- Referring to picture, place all objects on the sewing table.

- Pin and baste. The quilt hangs freely under hand and scissors and over border.

- Sew all pieces by hand or machine.

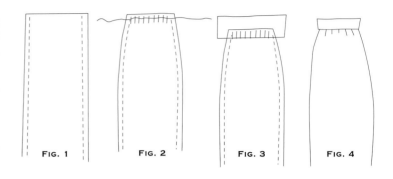

FIG. 1   FIG. 2   FIG. 3   FIG. 4

FIG. 6

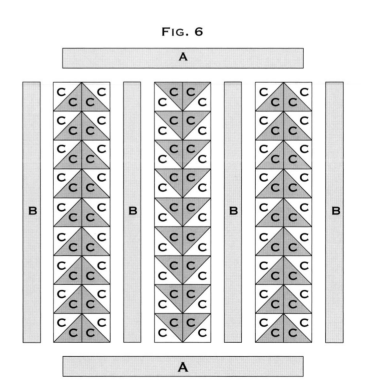

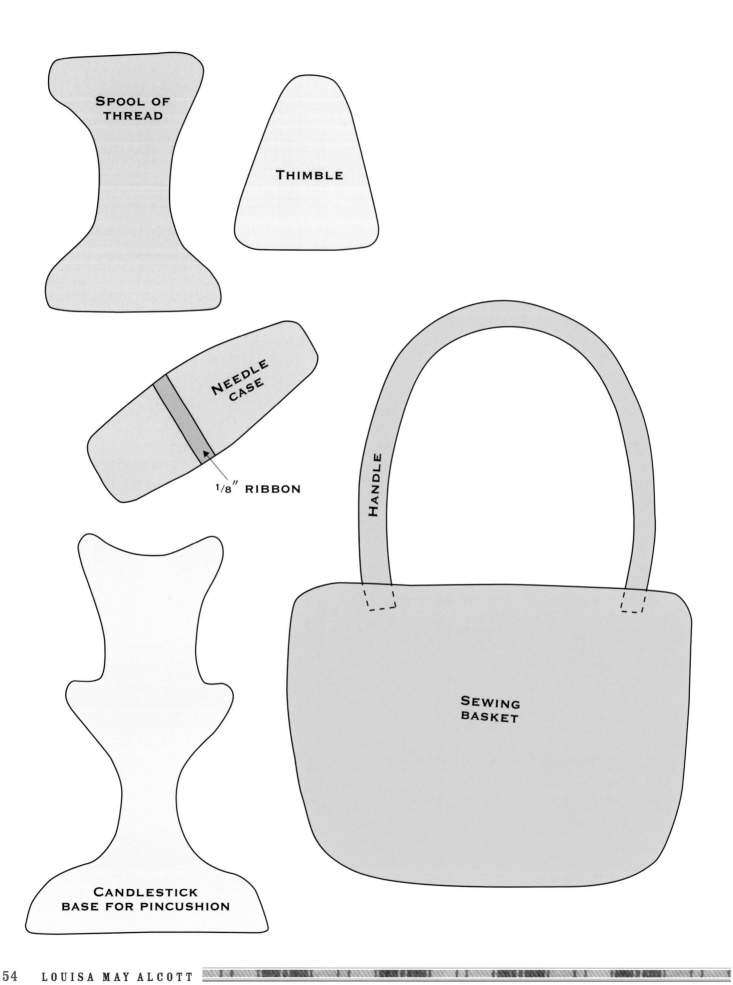

SPOOL OF
THREAD

THIMBLE

NEEDLE
CASE

1/8" RIBBON

HANDLE

SEWING
BASKET

CANDLESTICK
BASE FOR PINCUSHION

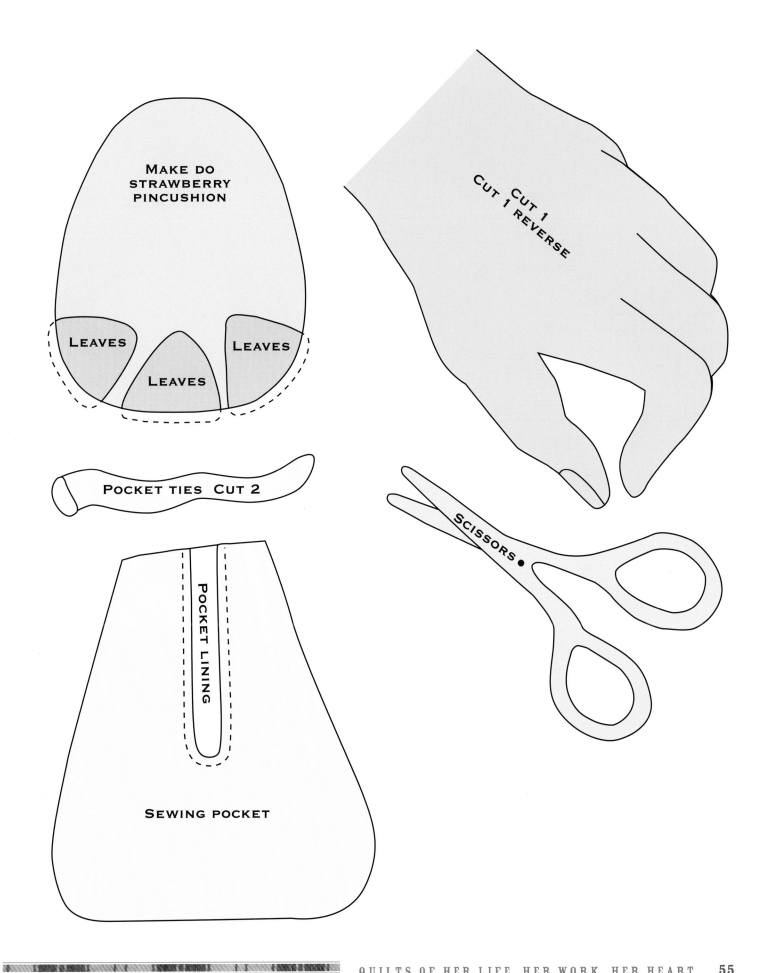

MAKE DO
STRAWBERRY
PINCUSHION

LEAVES

LEAVES

LEAVES

POCKET TIES CUT 2

POCKET LINING

SEWING POCKET

CUT 1
CUT 1 REVERSE

SCISSORS ●

"I can't fight, but I can nurse."
— Union Hotel Hospital, Washington D.C.

Louisa wrote letters for the soldiers and sent letters to families of the dying men. This hospital scene shows her in a brown cotton dress and apron, her yard long hair in a bun. The Soldier lies in his bed of ticking sheets with a quilt over his sick body. He has typhoid fever and one hand. Many soldiers had their hands shot off as they raised them to reload their rifles in the heat of battle. The blond night nurse complains of the cold air as it comes in thru the window Louisa has just opened. She believes in fresh air to help restore good health.

Louisa longed to join the Union struggle in any way a woman could. She was moved by a call for nurses at the Union Hotel Hospital in Washington, DC in 1863. The following describes in her own words her ordeal and compassion for the wounded and dying soldiers on the Union Army.[1]

- Ednah D. Cheney

1859 September. – *Great State Encampment here. Town full of soldiers, with military fuss and feathers. I like a camp, and long for a war, to see how it all seems. I can't fight, but I can nurse. [Prophetic again. – L.M.A.]*

Journal kept at the Hospital, Georgetown, D.C., 1862.

November. – *Thirty years old. Decided to go to Washington as nurse if I could find a place. Help needed, and I love nursing, and must let out my pent-up energy in some new way. Winter is always a hard and a dull time, and if I am away there is one less to feed and warm and worry over.*

I want new experiences, and am sure to get'em if I go. So I've sent in my name, and bide my time writing tales, to leave all snug behind me, and mending up my old clothes, - for nurses don't need nice things, thank Heaven!

– Louisa May Alcott

"I can't fight, but I can nurse."
– Union Hotel Hospital, Washington D.C.

Yardage

BACKGROUND

- Wallpaper –18 ¼″ x 23″ green striped ticking
- Floor – 5 ¼″ x 23″ blue ticking

APPLIQUÉS

- Louisa's dress – 9″ x 11″ of brown/pink calico
- Apron and ties – 6″ x 8″ pink calico print
- Hair – 3″ x 3″ brown
- Face and hands – 3″ x 3″ flesh tone solid fabric
- Soldiers face – 2″ x 2″ yellow tone
  (he has pneumonia)
- Soldiers night shirt and cap – 8″ x 8″ of shirting
- Soldiers beard and hair – 3″ x 3″ reddish brown
- Soldiers bed – 7″ x 7″ tan homespun or rough
  looking woven fabric.
- Soldiers pillow – 6″ x 8″ yellow ticking
- Writing table – 5″ x 8″ dark brown moiré
- Letter – 3″ x 3″ linen or muslin
- Pen – 2″ x 3″ black
- Towels and cots – ½ of ⅛ yard of plain small white
  strips, ticking or shirting
- Pillows – 3″ x 9″ Civil war print or flags
- Windows – 2 – 4 ½″ x 8″ of dark blue moiré
  or night sky fabric
- Wood window trim – 8″ x 8″ dark brown moiré

CIVIL WAR NURSE

- Dress – 7″ x 8″ calico print
- Apron – 4″ x 4″ of blue ticking
- Sleeves – 4″ x 4″ of indigo blue print

- Shoes – scrap of black 2″ x 2″
- Hair – 2 ½″ x 2 ½″ gold or yellow
- Hands and face – 3″ x 3″ of flesh tone
- Undersleeves – 2″ x 4″ light off white or shirting

9″ QUILT BLOCK

- ½ fat ¼ of a dark print
- ½ fat ¼ of medium flannel

Sewing Directions

Add ¼″ seam allowance to all appliqué patterns.

- Sew the floor fabric strip to the wall fabric for the
  background block. Press seam.
- Referring to the General Directions cut out octagon
  background block.
- Sew border strips around octagon.

Pieced Quilt

- Cut 20 light 1 ½″ squares A
- Cut 16 dark 1 ½″ squares A
- Cut 8 dark 1 ½″ x 3 ½″ rectangles B
- Cut 4 light 1 ½″ x 3 ½″ rectangles B
- Cut 1 light 3 ½″ square C
- Assemble the 9″ quilt according to the key.
  See Figure 1.
- Prepare all appliqués for hand or machine sewing.
- Ink the faces of all 3 people attach hair and beard.
- Assemble head, dress, apron, faces and hands of the 2 women.
- Dress the soldier – his hand was shot off while he was reloading his rifle, therefore, no hand included. Poor man.
- Referring to the picture, place the bed sheet on the background. Place the pillow at the top of the sheet place the soldier with head on pillow and shirt on sheet. Tuck the quilt block under his arm. Let the quilt and pillow lay over the border. The bottom and right side of quilt hang loose and unsewn to the block as shown in picture. Pin in place.
- Place the letter and pen upon the table, and set between Louisa and soldier.
- Sew window frames to blue fabric and place at top of block.
- Sew pillowcases to cots and place around the room.
- Place the nurse after block #7 and #8 are sewn together, as her arm and part of her dress lay over the borders.
- When all figures are placed to your liking, sew each figure to block.

FIG. 1

A	A	A	B	A	A	A
A	A	A	B	A	A	A
A	A	A	B	A	A	A
B	B	B	C	B	B	B
A	A	A	B	A	A	A
A	A	A	B	A	A	A
A	A	A	B	A	A	A

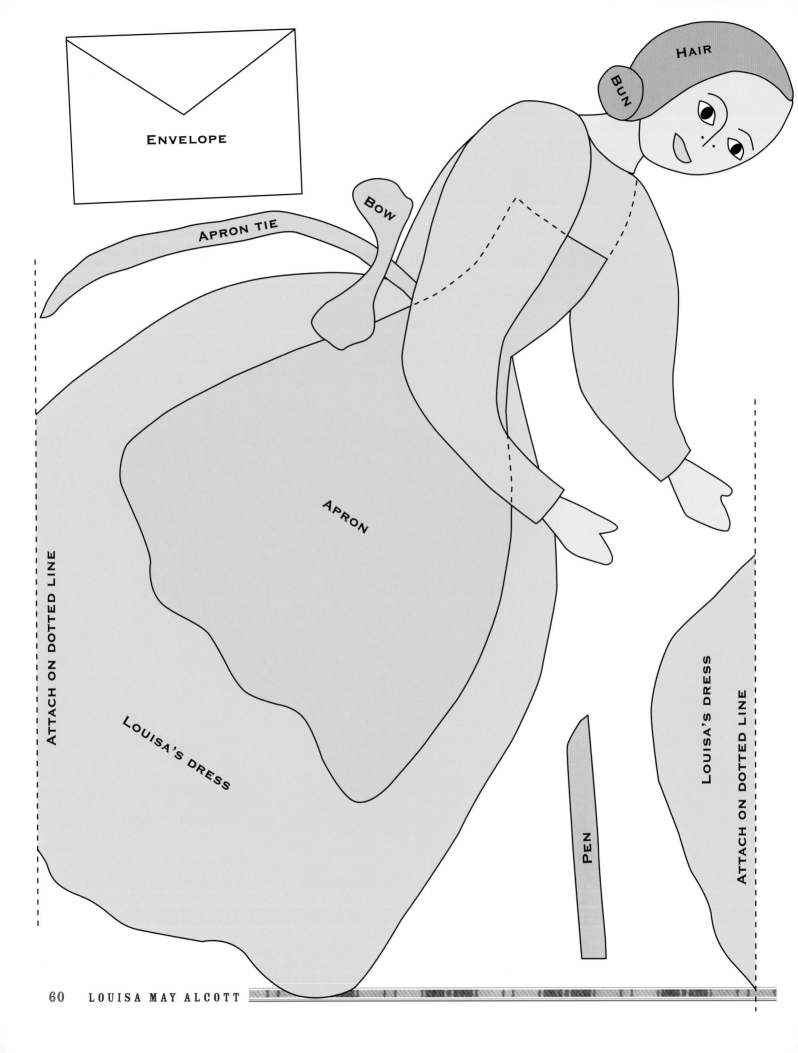

ENVELOPE

BOW

APRON TIE

HAIR

BUN

APRON

ATTACH ON DOTTED LINE

LOUISA'S DRESS

LOUISA'S DRESS

ATTACH ON DOTTED LINE

PEN

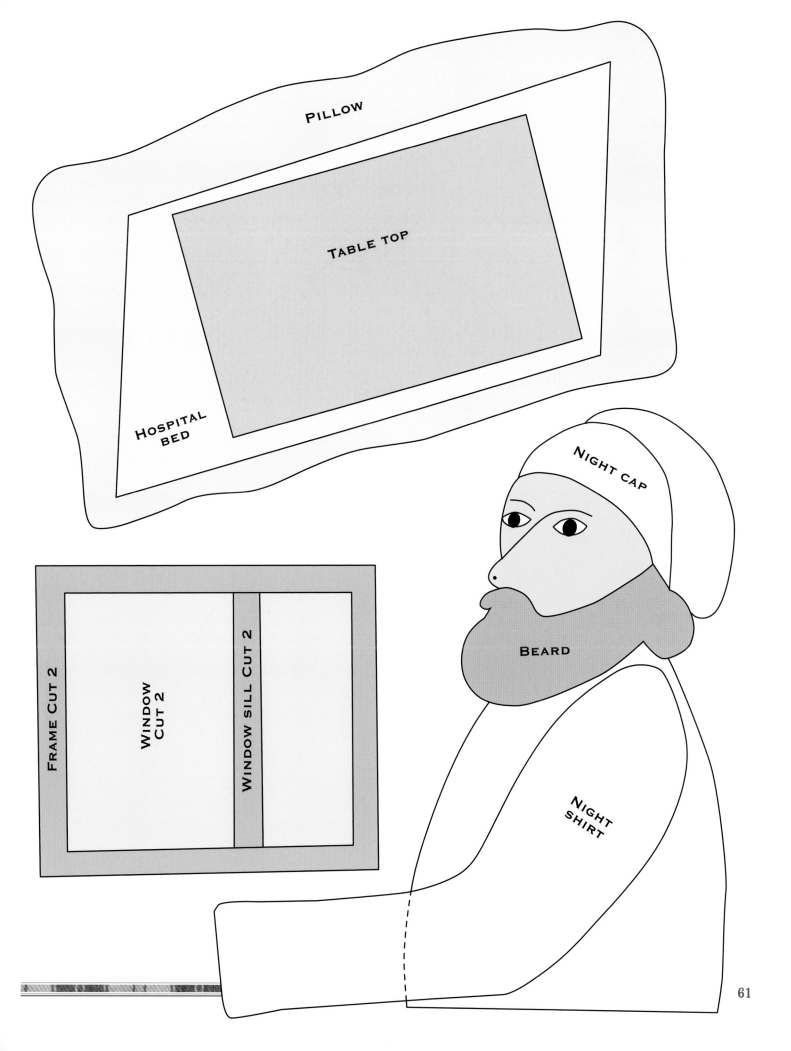

PILLOW

TABLE TOP

HOSPITAL
BED

NIGHT CAP

FRAME CUT 2

WINDOW
CUT 2

WINDOW SILL CUT 2

BEARD

NIGHT
SHIRT

61

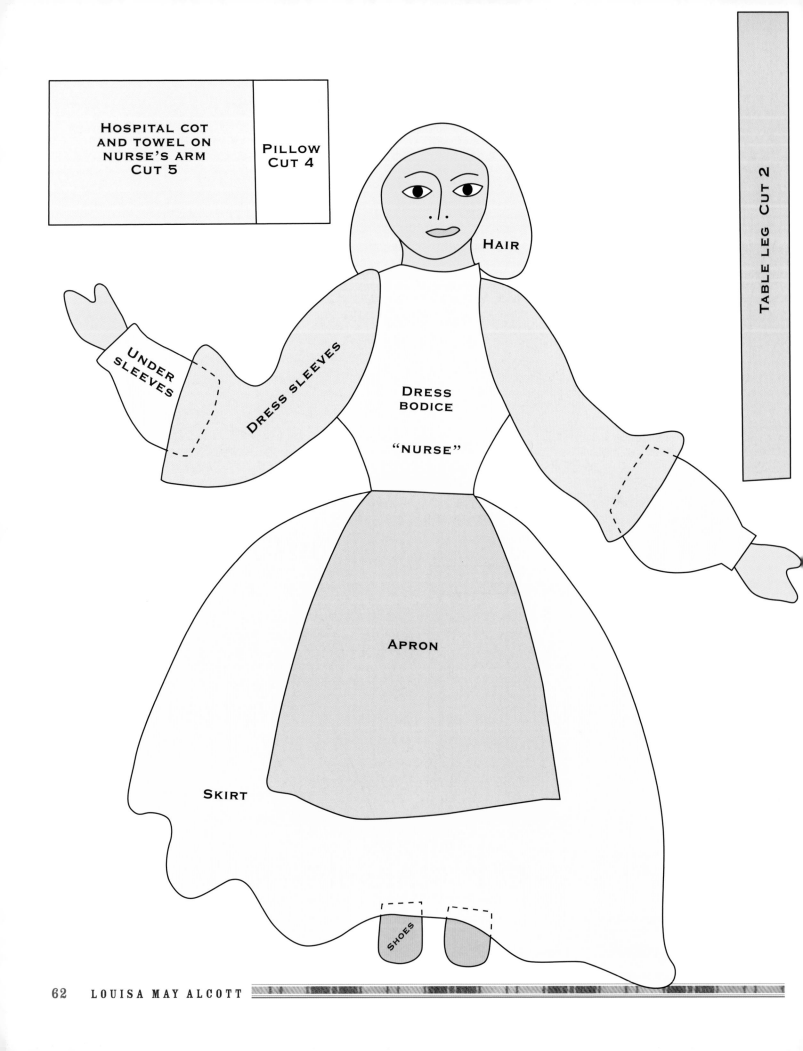

HOSPITAL COT
AND TOWEL ON
NURSE'S ARM
CUT 5

PILLOW
CUT 4

TABLE LEG CUT 2

HAIR

UNDER
SLEEVES

DRESS SLEEVES

DRESS
BODICE

"NURSE"

APRON

SKIRT

SHOES

4 Pieced Setting Blocks

Pictures of the setting blocks can be found on pages 68-69.

The 4 pieced setting blocks are – 10″ finished.

Yardage is for all 4 pieced blocks

- ⅓ yard dark plaid
- ⅓ yard yellow check
- ⅛ yard red print calico
- ⅛ yard brown print calico

Pinwheel

CUTTING & SEWING DIRECTIONS

- A - Cut 8 red and 2 yellow 2 ⅛″ squares

- B - Cut 4 brown and 4 yellow 2 ½″ squares. Cut on the diagonal to end with 8 brown and 8 yellow triangles. *See Figure 1.*

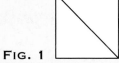

FIG. 1

- C – Cut 2 dark plaid 5 ½″ squares

- Referring to *Figure 2* piece 2 Pinwheel blocks.

- Sew Pinwheel blocks to 5 ½″ squares C to make a 4 Patch 10″ finished block.

Pinwheel Variation

CUTTING & SEWING DIRECTIONS

- A - Cut 2 dark plaid and 2 yellow 5 ⅞″ squares. Cut on the diagonal to end with 4 dark plaid and 4 yellow triangles. *See Figure 1.*

- Referring to *Figure 2* piece the block.

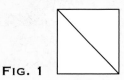

FIG. 1

9 Patch

CUTTING & SEWING DIRECTIONS

- A - Cut 5 dark plaid and 4 yellow 3 ⅞″ squares

- Referring to *Figure 1* piece the block.

Double 9 Patch

CUTTING & SEWING DIRECTIONS

- A - Cut 8 red, 8 yellow and 2 brown 2 ⅛″ squares

- B - Cut 2 dark plaid 5 ½″ squares

- Referring to *Figure 1* piece 2 Nine Patch blocks.

- Sew Nine Patch blocks to 5 ½″ squares B to make a 4 Patch 10″ finished block.

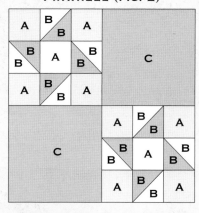

PINWHEEL (FIG. 2)

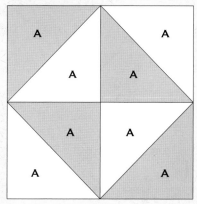

PINWHEEL VARIATION (FIG. 2)

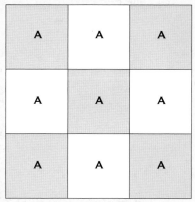

NINE PATCH (FIG. 1)

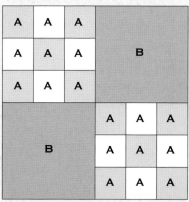

DOUBLE NINE PATCH (FIG. 1)

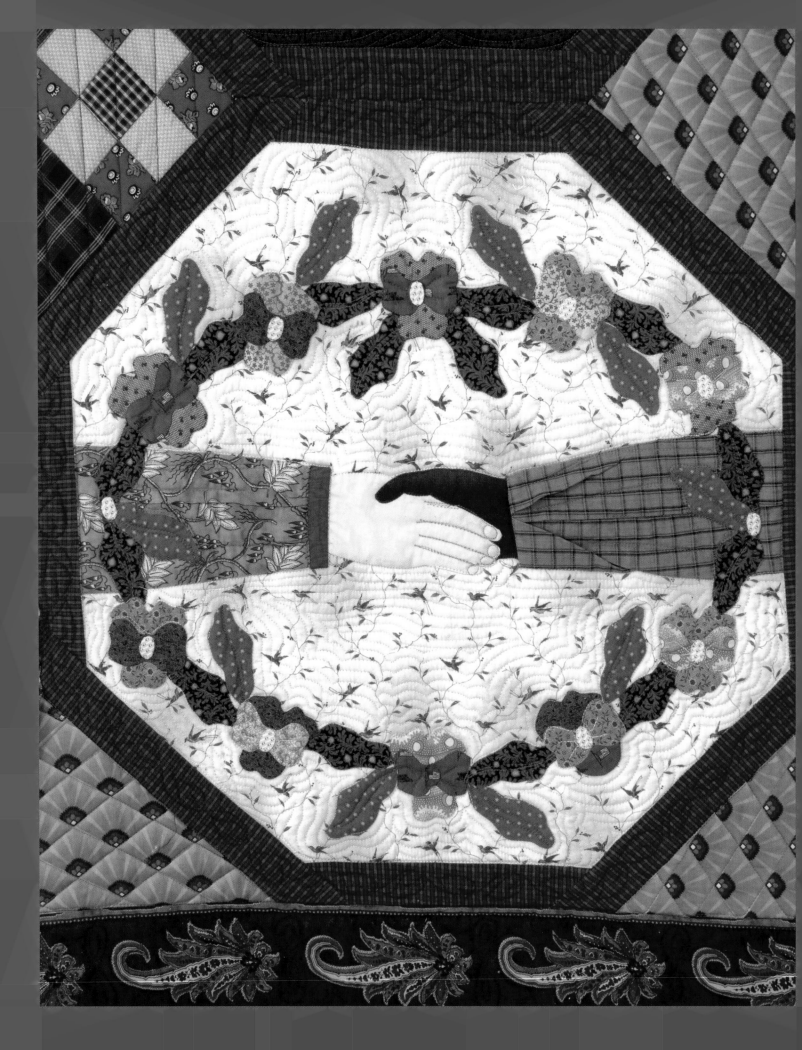

"Union Forever - Heartsease"

The two clasping hands belong to Louisa and the runaway slaves she and her family assisted. At the end of the war the Union stood and I made a wreath of "Heartsease", an old name for pansy. At the ending of the war, everyones hearts were heavy for the terrible loss of life-finally their hearts were at ease. I began the "Louisa" quilt in 2002 with this block of pansies and clasping hands. I let my idea for a story quilt "simmer" until I found her journal, and that gave me the insight into how to portray Louisa.

After leaving the duties of nursing behind, Louisa returned home to her family where she almost died from her treatment for typhoid fever, A medicine used to treat the disease contained mercury and Louisa declined into ill health and never recovered. She died two days after her father's death, March 6, 1888.[1]

– *Ednah D. Cheney*

1863 February. – *Recovered my senses after three weeks of delirium, and was told I had had a very bad typhoid fever, had nearly died, and was still very sick. All of which seemed rather curious, for I remembered nothing of it. Found a queer, thin, big-eyed face when I looked in the glass; didn't know myself at all; and when I tried to walk discovered that I couldn't and cried because my legs wouldn't go.*

People sent letters, money, kind inquiries, and goodies for the old "Nuss." I tried to sew, read, and write, and found I had to begin all over again. Received $10 for my labors in Washington. Had all my hair, a yard and a half long, cut off, and went into caps like a grandma. Felt badly about losing my one beauty. Never mind, it might have been my head, and a wig outside is better than a loss of wits inside.

1863 May. - *Went to Readville, and saw the 54th Colored Regiment, both there and next day in town as they left for the South. Enjoyed it very much; also the Antislavery meetings.*

– *Louisa May Alcott*

Yardage

BACKGROUND

- 23″ x 23″ square of one solid piece of a neutral tone print

APPLIQUÉS

- Hand on left - 3 ½″ x 6″ of a light flesh tone
- Hand on right - 3 ½″ x 5″ of a dark brown tone.
- Left sleeve – 5″ x 8″ of a blue print
- Right sleeve - 5″ x 9″ of a blue homespun plaid
- Cuff on left sleeve - 1″ x 3 ½″
- 10 Pansies – use several different pink and purple calicos for the petals that are at least 3 ½″ x 3 ½″
- 10 Centers of Pansies – 4″ x 4″ square of yellow
- 24 Leaves – 10 light, and 14 dark green – ⅛ yard each color

Sewing Directions:

Add ¼″ seam allowance to all appliqué patterns.

NOTE: On this block sew octagon borders after sleeves are placed against raw edge of block.

- Referring to the General Directions cut out octagon background block.
- Prepare all appliqués for hand or machine sewing.
- Ink or embroider lines between the fingers of left hand.
- Assemble "Heartsease" (pansies).
- For the left sleeve, cut 1 blue print rectangle 5″ x 8″ – Turn under ¼″ on each long side and baste. *See Figure 1.*
- Gather 1 end of sleeve to 3″. *See Figure 2.*

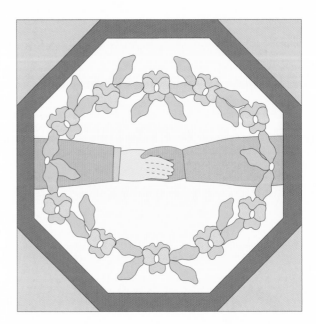

- For the cuff, cut a 1″ x 3 ½″ rectangle. With right sides together sew 1 side of cuff to 3″ gathered sleeve. *See Figure 3.*
- Fold cuff over seam and press. Turn cuff edges under ¼″ and press. Fold in sides of cuff even with sleeve, press and baste all edges of the cuff. *See Figure 4.*
- Attach to hand.
- For the right sleeve, cut a 5″ x 9″ rectangle. Turn under ¼″ on all sides and baste. *See Figure 5.*
- Fold a pleat at the top of sleeve and fold corners under to make a 3″ sleeve end. Baste across top of sleeve to hold pleat and folds. *See Figure 6.*
- Attach hand. Place clasping hands as shown, with sleeves touching opposite sides of block against raw edge and sew in place.
- After sleeves and hands are sewn in place, pin and baste the "Heartsease" (pansy) and leaves as shown. Sew in place.
- Sew border strips around octagon.

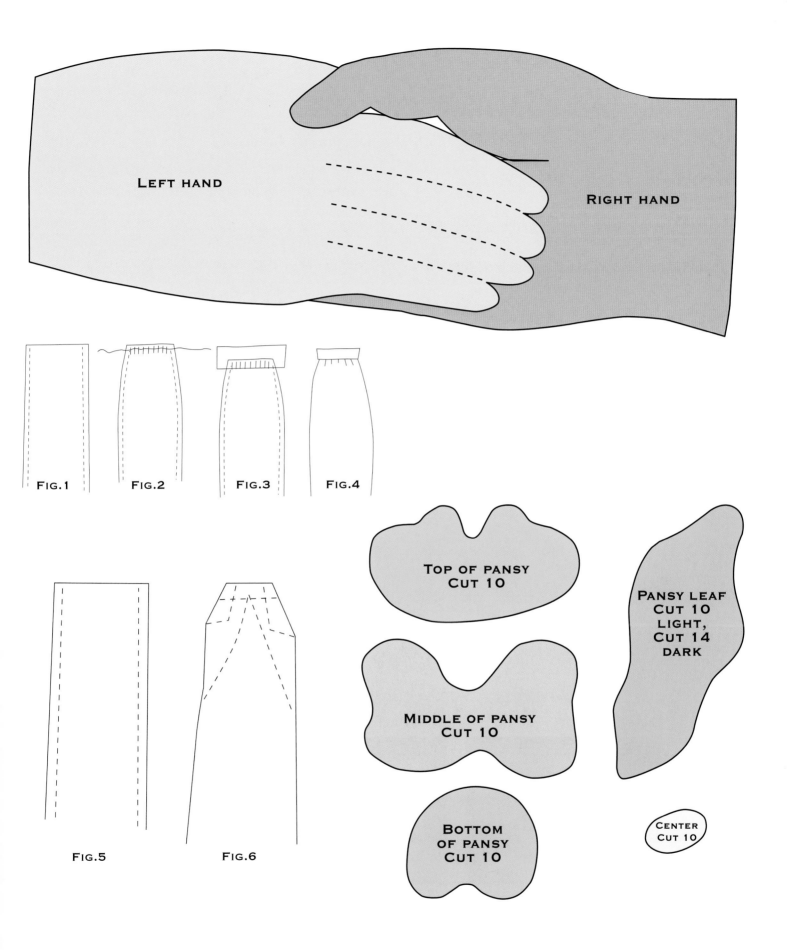

LEFT HAND

RIGHT HAND

FIG.1   FIG.2   FIG.3   FIG.4

FIG.5   FIG.6

TOP OF PANSY
CUT 10

PANSY LEAF
CUT 10
LIGHT,
CUT 14
DARK

MIDDLE OF PANSY
CUT 10

BOTTOM
OF PANSY
CUT 10

CENTER
CUT 10

Setting The Quilt Together

After all 9 appliqué blocks and the 4 pieced blocks are completed you may begin the setting process.

Yardage

SETTING/CORNER TRIANGLES: ¾ yard blue print. You want the block borders to stand out, so choose a color that will compliment the block borders.

QUILT BORDERS: 3 ½ yards of a large printed stripe or paisley.

Cutting Directions

OUTSIDE SETTING TRIANGLES: 8

- Cut 2 - 15 ½" squares of the blue print.

- Cut on both diagonals to end with 4 triangles per square (total of 8 triangles). *See Figure 1.*

CORNER TRIANGLES: 4

- Cut 2 - 8" squares of the blue print.

- Cut on the diagonal to end with 2 triangles per square (total of 4 triangles). *See Figure 2.*

FIG. 1

FIG. 2

Setting The Quilt

CREATING ROWS: *See Figure 3.*

Leave a ¼" open seam at both ends of the blocks you are sewing together in order to set in the pieced blocks and setting triangles later.

Create Row 1 by sewing:

- Block 1's right border to block 2's left border. Then sew block 2's right border to block 3's left border.

Create Row 2 by sewing:

- Block 4's right border to block 5's left border. Then sew block 5's right border to block 6's left border.

Create Row 3 by sewing:

- Block 7's right border to block 8's left border. Then sew block 8's right border to block 9's left border. Pin and sew the nurse from block 8 over the border between block 7 & 8.

Setting Rows

- Start with the bottom of row 1. Set the first pieced block between block 1's lower right and block 2's lower left borders. Sew the two sides of the pieced block to the borders finishing the seams.

- Repeat the process for the second pieced block between block 2's lower right and block 3's lower left borders.

- Repeat these steps to set the 3rd and 4th pieced blocks to the bottom of row 2.

PINWHEEL

PINWHEEL VARIATION

NINE PATCH

- Sew block 1's bottom border to block 4's top border. Set in the second half of the first pieced block. Sew block 2's bottom border to block 5' top border. Set in the second half of the second pieced block. Sew the block 3's bottom border to block 6's top border.

- Repeat the above step to attach rows 2 and 3 and pieced blocks 3 and 4.

Setting Corner and Side Triangles

- Sew one blue corner triangle to block 1's upper left border. Sew one corner triangle to the upper right border of block 3. Sew one corner triangle to block 7's lower left border. Sew one corner triangle to the lower right border of block 9.

- Pin one large blue side triangle between block 1's upper right and block 2's upper left borders with the point of the triangle meeting in the ¼″ open seam allowance of the two borders. Repeat, inserting a side triangle between block 2's upper right and block 3's upper left border. Repeat inserting side triangles between blocks on the sides and bottom of quilt.

- Appliqué all remaining loose block pieces to the background.

DOUBLE NINE PATCH

Quilt Borders

10″ finished borders - Measure your quilt and cut borders to fit.

- Cut the upper and lower borders 10 ½″ x 72 ½″. Attach to quilt.

- Cut the two side borders 10 ½″ x 92 ½″. Attach to quilt.

- Quilt and bind.

FIG. 3

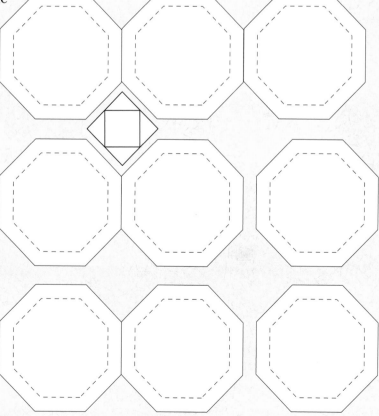

CONCORD, MASSACHUSETTS

50˝ X 50˝

L ouisa grew up surrounded by her parents' friends who were intellectuals, authors, abolitionist, and notable women who lectured and campaigned for women's rights. I have numbered and named each house after friends who lived in Concord or who visited the Alcotts' "Orchard House."

The fabrics I chose are Civil War era reproductions fabrics from Moda. The calicos, plaids and checks are in shades of red, purple, blue, brown and yellow for the houses and flowers. Look for contrasting plain or moirés for the house "beams" and the tulip blossoms. For the clumps of flowers around the houses, look for prints that have trailing stems with flowers for a "cut out chintz" look. The background squares were made with a simple, none distracting woven fabric that looks like ½″ squares.

Yardage

Plain or Moire fabrics are interchangeable, and all windows, doors, and chimneys are made from scraps left from cutting houses.

Ralph Waldo Emerson House #1

- 1 fat ¼ each of blue print and light brown plain or moiré
- Roof - 1 fat ¼ brown print

Nathaniel and Sophia Hawthorne House #2

- 1 fat ¼ each of a red print, brown print and plain red
- Roof - 1 fat ¼ of dark brown print

Margaret Fuller House #3

- 1 fat ¼ each of a light purple print and dark purple print, and a plain purple
- Roof - 1 fat ¼ of a light purple print

Alcott Orchard House #4

- 1 fat ¼ each of a brown plaid, a brown/yellow check and a light yellow calico
- Roof - 1 fat ¼ of a red paisley or large print

Ellery Channing House #5

- 1 fat ¼ each of 1 yellow floral and 1 blue floral print and 1 plain yellow
- Roof - 1 fat ¼ of a light yellow print

Henry David Thoreau House #6

- 1 fat ¼ each of 1 dark red print, 1 dark brown print
- Roof - 1 fat ¼ of a dark red print

Horace and Mary Mann House #7

- 1 fat ¼ each of 1 dark red print, 1 medium brown print, and 1 dark brown plain
- Roof - 1 fat ¼ of a medium blue print

Oliver Wendell Holmes House #8

- 1 fat ¼ each of a purple plaid and light purple print
- Roof - 1 scrap of large yellow and purple print

Additional Yardage and Supplies

- 1 ¾ yards of a dull gold, woven fabric for 4- 20 ½" background squares and house windows
- 1 fat ¼ of plain ecru for the picket fence
- Scraps of thin red and white stripes 2 ½" x 4 ¾" for flag
- Scraps of blue 1 ¾" x 2" for the canton
- Scrap of brown 1" x 9 ½" for the pole
- Scrap of blue for the stand
- ½ yard green for 4 - 1" bias stems
- Scraps of prints that have trailing stems with flowers for a "cut out chintz" look for the clumps/bushes of flowers around the houses
- ¼ yard light print for 1" finished narrow border.
- ⅝ yard dark print for 4" finished border
- 1" Clover Bias Maker

Cutting Directions

¼" seam allowance is included in the rotary cutting measurements, ¼" seam allowance will need to be added to all templates. Refer to picture of quilt for color placement and *Figure #1* for house assembly.

For each house:

1, 2, 3, 5, 6 and 7 - House #5 reverse the order of beams and corner beam. Refer to picture.

- Cut 6 Beams 'A'- 1 ½" x 10 ½" strips alternating light and dark colors red/brown, yellow/blue etc.
- Cut 1 'B' Roof add ¼" seam allowance to template.
- Cut 1 Corner Beam 'D' - 1 ½" x 8 ½"
- Cut 1 Beam 'E' - 2 ½" x 10 ½"

Doors, Window and Chimneys:

- Cut 6 Doors 2 ¼" x 3 ¼" plain dark brown
- Cut 12 Windows 1 ½" x 1 ¾" light tan
- Cut 12 Chimneys 1 ½" squares plain dark red

House #4

- Cut 1 'F' roof add ¼" seam allowance to template
- Cut 3 light print and 3 dark plaid strips 1 ½" x 11 ½"
- Cut 2 dark check strips 2 ½" x 11 ½"
- Cut 4 Windows 1 ¾" x 4" dark red
- Cut 1 Chimney 1 ¾" x 2 ¼" plain medium brown

House #8

- Cut 1 'B' roof add ¼" seam allowance to template
- Cut 2 light print and 2 dark print strips 'A' 1 ½" x 10 ½"
- Cut 3 dark plaid strips 'E' 2 ½" x10 ½"
- Cut 1 purple corner beam 1 ½" x 10 ½"
- Cut 1 Door 3 ½" x 3 ½" plain dark red. Round off top corners for an arched door.
- Cut 3 Windows 1 ½" x 2 ½" plain dark red
- Cut 1 Chimney 1 ½" x 2 ¼" plain dark red

Bias Stems:

- Cut 4 - 1" x 21" bias strips for stems
- Use your 1" Clover bias maker to turn under the raw edge seam allowance, gently press the turned edges as you pull through the bias maker.

Tulips

- Cut 12 - 3 ½" x 5 ½" strips of a floral print, and another 12 - 3 ½" x 5 ½" strips of plain fabric from the leftover fat ¼'s used for the houses.
- Sew strips together with a ¼" seam.

- Place flower template 'G' over seam and cut ¼″ around flower.

Flower Bushes:

- Cut 10 free form shapes from prints that have trailing stems with flowers for a "cut out chintz" look.

Picket Fence:

Cut on straight grain, not bias

- Cut 15 - 1″ x 3 ½″ strips of ecru for pickets and arch.

- Cut 2 - 1″ x 4″ strips of ecru for the end posts.

- Cut 2 - 1″ x 17 ½″ long strips for two long fence rails.

- Pre-baste raw edges of posts and rails to make placement and appliqué easier and accurate.

Flag and Pole:

- Cut 1 - 2 ½″ x 4 ¾″ rectangle from red and white stripe fabric.

- Cut 1 - 1 ¾″ x 2″ rectangle from blue for the canton.

- Cut 1 - 1″ x 9 ½″ rectangle from brown for the pole.

- Cut 1 - 'H' from light blue fabric for the stand. Add ¼″ seam allowance to the template.

Background Squares:

- Cut 4 - 20 ½″ squares.

Sewing Directions

- Sew beams together to create the house. Refer to the picture of the quilt to help assemble each house.

- Appliqué "corner beam" 'D' to the house.

- Appliqué doors and windows to houses with a black thread in a running stitch. Use perle cotton or quilting thread, so the stitches show.

- Lay out your 4 background blocks and place two houses on each background in positions that create a circle around the town square. Pin in place.

- Place the chimneys for each house and pin in place. Appliqué the houses and chimneys to the background blocks.

- Referring to the pictures appliqué the cut out bushes of flowers in place.

- Sew 4 blocks together.

- Sew canton to flag. Make small folds in the flag to create a waving flag. Sew middle fold to hold flag to background.

- Sew flagpole and stand in middle of the town square.

- The picket fence is placed between houses 2 and 3. Refer to the picture for placement. Layout the 2 long rail strips pin and baste in place.

- Place the 2 end posts at ends of rails. Pin and baste. Pin and baste posts on top of rails. Baste arch in middle of fence.

- Appliqué with a black thread in a running stitch. Use perle cotton or quilting thread, so the stitches show.

- The long stemmed flowers are placed next to the houses falling over the center seams. Refer to the picture as a placement guide, or arrange as you wish.

Borders

Refer to *Figure 2*

- Cut 2 borders 1 ½″ x 40 ½″ and 2 borders 1 ½″ x 42″. Sew borders to quilt.

- Cut 2 borders 4 ½″ x 42 ½″ and 2 borders 4 ½″ x 50 ½″. Sew borders to body of quilt.

- Quilt and Bind.

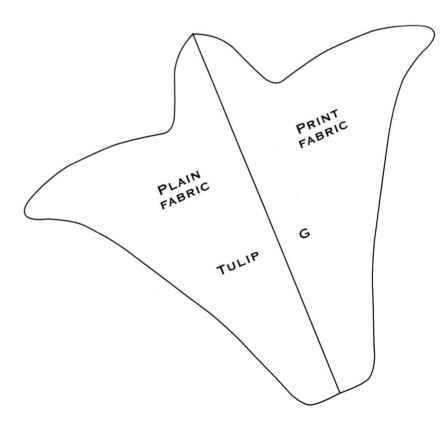

PRINT FABRIC

PLAIN FABRIC

TULIP

G

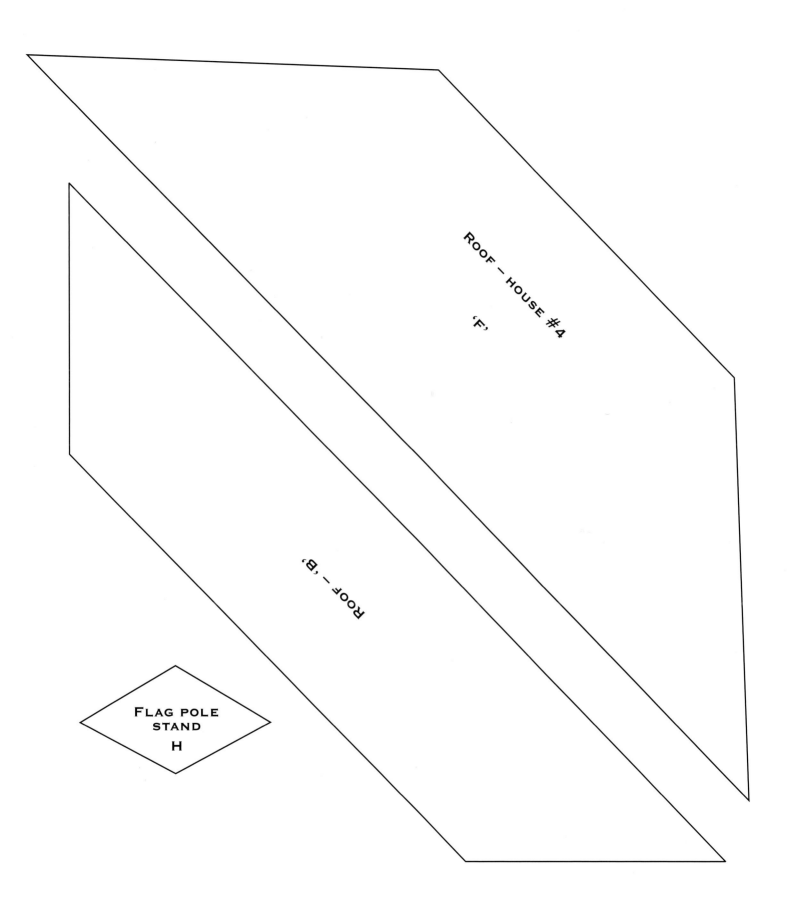

ROOF – HOUSE #4
'F'

ROOF – 'B'

FLAG POLE
STAND
H

FIG. 1

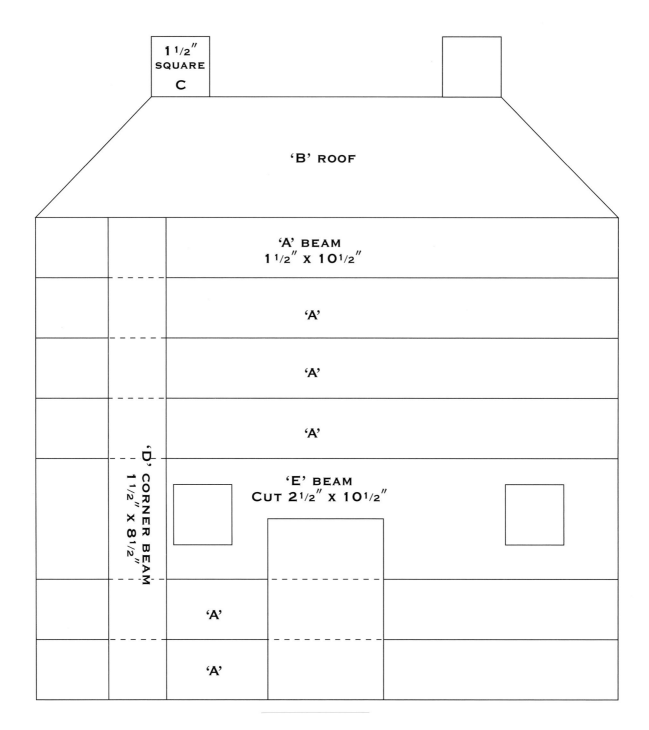

1 1/2″ SQUARE
C

'B' ROOF

'A' BEAM
1 1/2″ x 10 1/2″

'A'

'A'

'A'

'D' CORNER BEAM
1 1/2″ x 8 1/2″

'E' BEAM
CUT 2 1/2″ x 10 1/2″

'A'

'A'

FIG.2

50″ x 50″ FINISHED

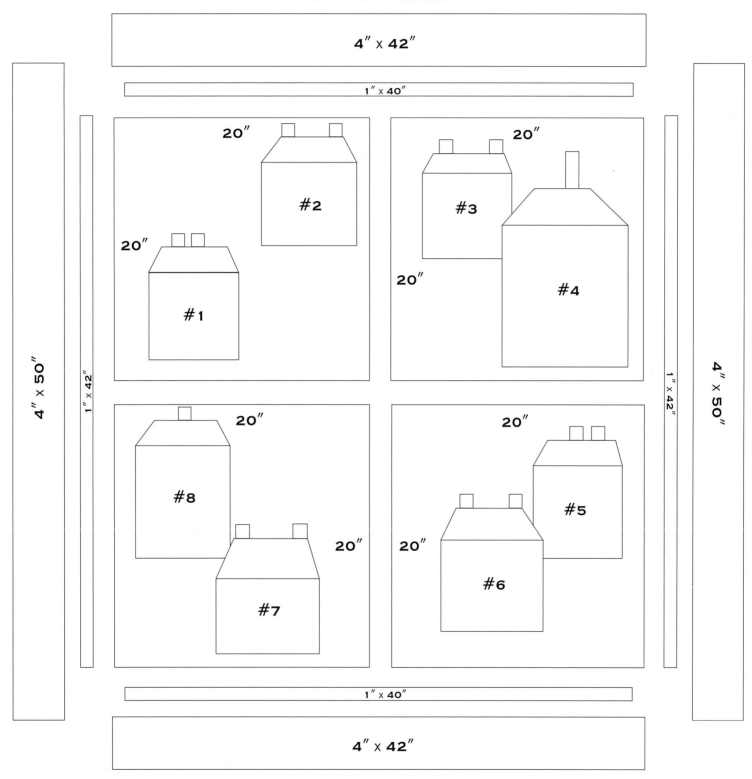

4″ x 42″

1″ x 40″

4″ x 50″

1″ x 42″

20″

20″

#2

20″

#1

20″

#3

20″

#4

20″

#8

20″

#7

20″

#5

20″

#6

1″ x 42″

4″ x 50″

1″ x 40″

4″ x 42″

FINISHED SIZES SHOWN

EAGLE SOLDIER'S QUILT

60˝ X 70˝

Eagle Soldier's Quilt

TO HONOR THE SOLDIERS WHO FOUGHT THE CIVIL WAR

Yardage

NINE PATCH BLOCKS 21 - 10″ FINISHED

- You may substitute scraps
- 1 ¼ yards total of blue plaids and solid
- 1 ¼ yards total of orange plaids and solid
- 2 ½ yards yellow/gold solid for 21 - 10″ finished alternate squares

Eagle

- ½ yard brown check or plaid for eagle wings and body
- ¼ yard ecru plaid or print for head and legs

Cannons

- ⅓ yard blue stripe or ticking for 2 cannons
- ⅛ yard black for cannon pieces and 10 cannon balls
- 3″ x 7″ red for cannon pieces
- 6″ x 10″ gold for cannon pieces

Sword

- 3″ x 12″ silver ironing board cover or silver fabric for blade
- 1″ x 2″ blue and white striped ticking for handle
- 5″ x 5″ gold for hilt and eagle feet

Halo around Eagle

- ⅔ yard of a plain contrasting color behind the eagle image that will show the eagle, cannons, and balls, and not blend into the quilt.
- Black perle cotton to sew running stitch around the eagle image.

Cutting Directions

NINE PATCH BLOCKS: for 21 blocks. These measurements include the ¼″ seam allowance

- Cut 105 - 3 ⅞″ blue squares
- Cut 84 - 3 ⅞″ oranges squares
- Cut 21 - 10 ½″ yellow/gold squares

EAGLE

Add ¼″ seam allowance to appliqué patterns

- Cut eagle's body and wings on the bias.
- Cut out all appliqués and prepare for hand or machine sewing.

Sewing Directions

- Assemble 21 Nine Patch blocks refer to *Figure 1.*
- Set blocks in rows, alternating pieced and plain squares. Refer to *Figure 2* for placement of blocks. The quilt is 7 rows of 6 blocks.
- Appliqué the top & bottom pieces of the cannons.
- Embroider or ink the eagle's eye.
- Appliqué the eagle's head to the body.
- Sew the wings to body of eagle.
- Appliqué legs to feet.
- Sew legs to the bottom of eagle's body.
- Place the two cannons under the legs & feet and baste in place.
- Place finished sword under eagle's feet, basting in place.
- Appliqué the feet, legs and sword to center of cannons. All eagle parts and cannons should be

FIG.1

FIG.2

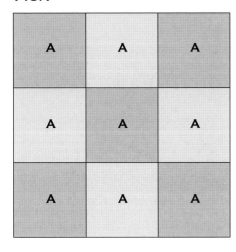

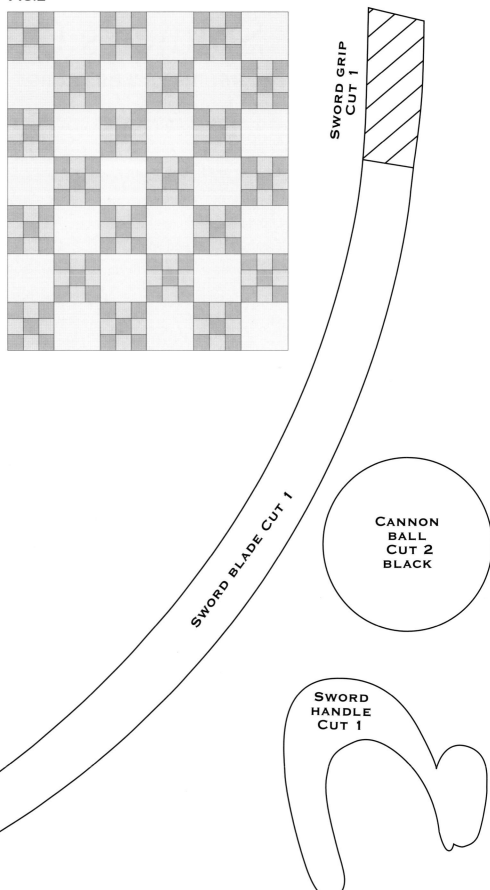

sewn together at this point.

- Lay out the 2/3 yards brown halo yardage on a table. This "halo" around the eagle image allows it to stand out from the pieced background and not blend into the pieced quilt.

- Referring to the picture place the eagle, cannons and 10 cannon balls on the brown yardage. Pin and baste eagle, cannons and cannon balls in place.

- Appliqué the eagle and all to the halo fabric.

- Cut halo out 1″ or so around entire image.

- Appliqué, using black perle cotton and a running stitch, the halo a little above center of the quilt.

- Bind edges of quilt.

- Tie into a "Comforter" or quilt by hand or machine.

SWORD GRIP CUT 1

SWORD BLADE CUT 1

CANNON BALL CUT 2 BLACK

SWORD HANDLE CUT 1

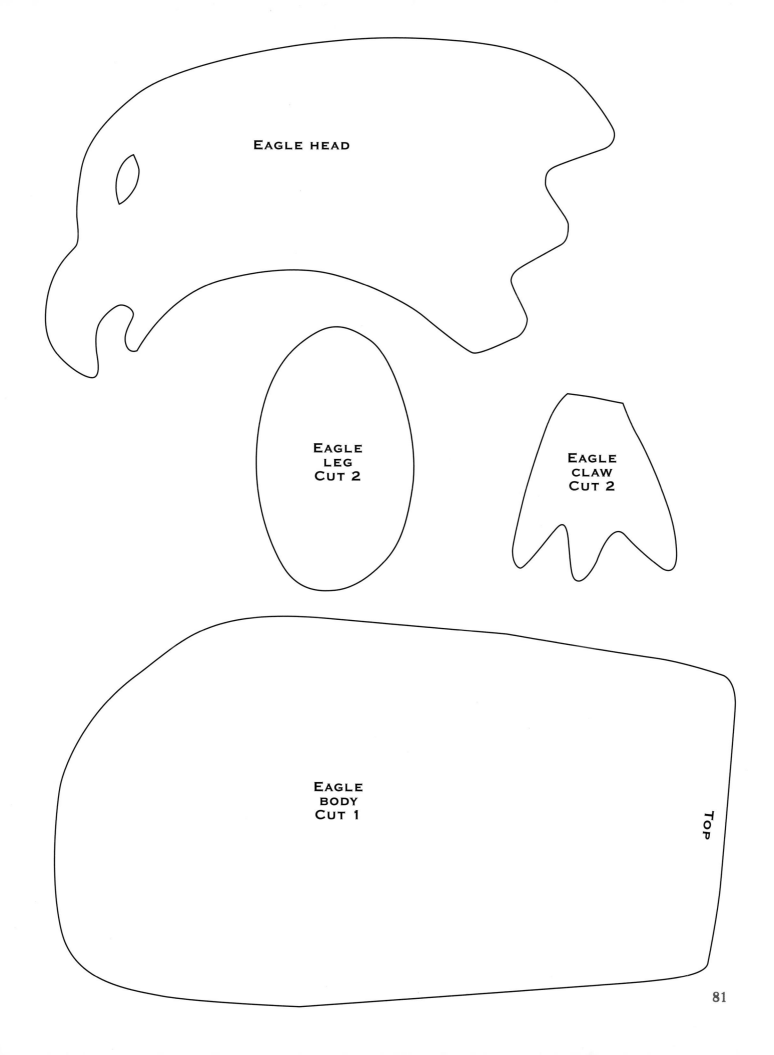

EAGLE HEAD

EAGLE
LEG
CUT 2

EAGLE
CLAW
CUT 2

EAGLE
BODY
CUT 1

TOP

81

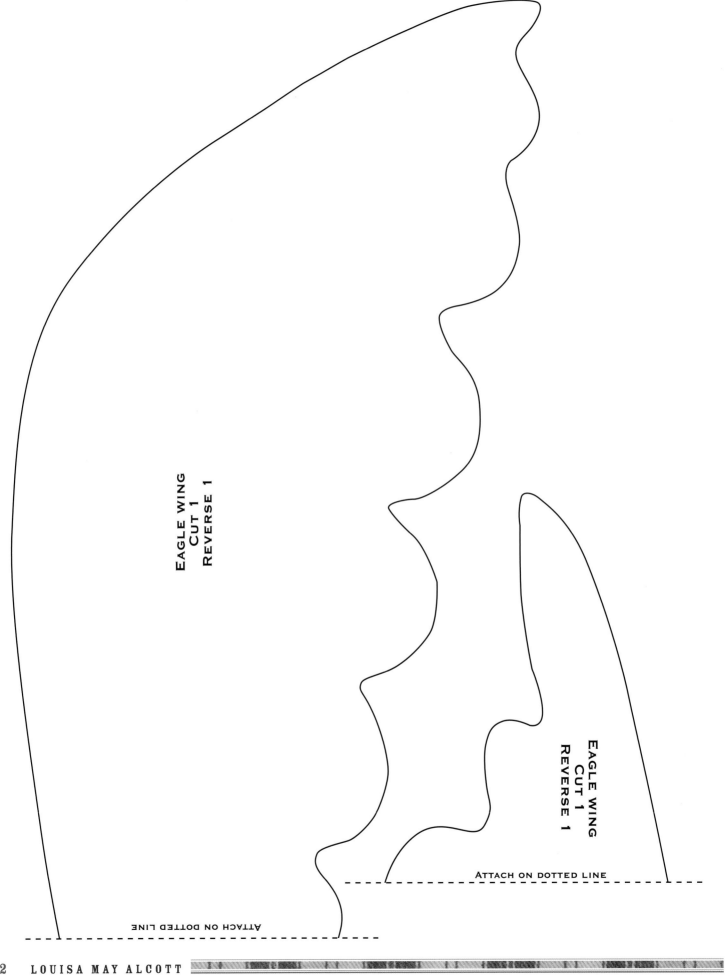

EAGLE WING
CUT 1
REVERSE 1

EAGLE WING
CUT 1
REVERSE 1

ATTACH ON DOTTED LINE

ATTACH ON DOTTED LINE

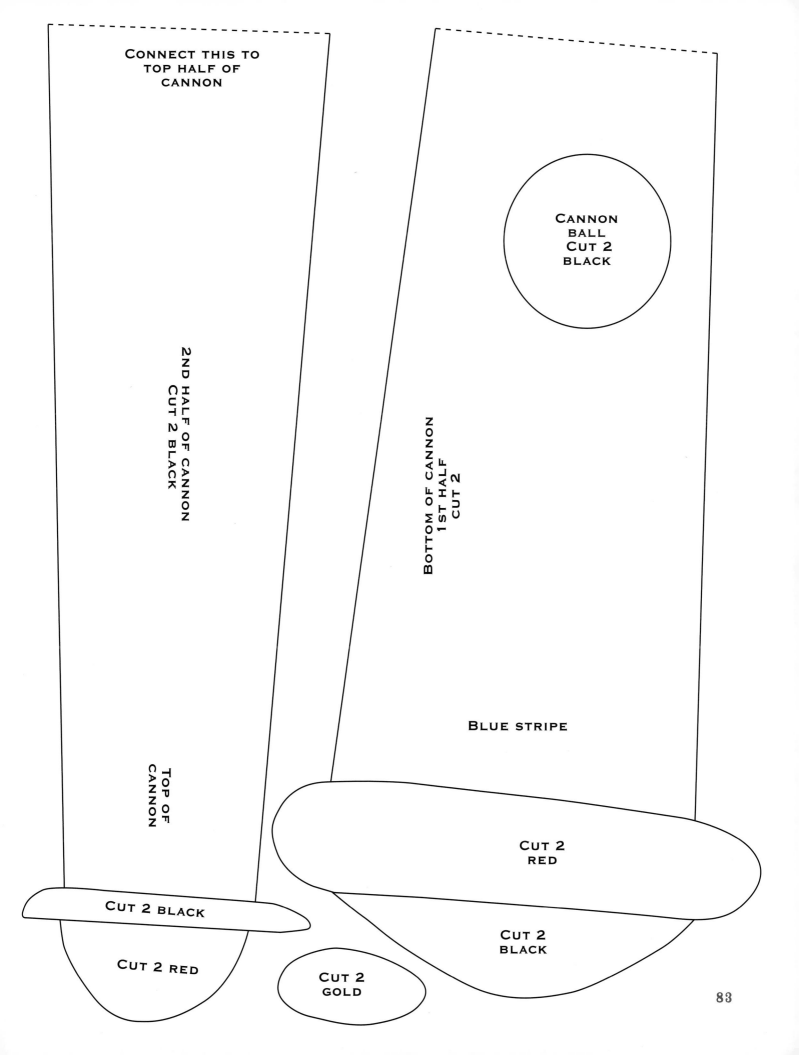

CONNECT THIS TO
TOP HALF OF
CANNON

2ND HALF OF CANNON
CUT 2 BLACK

TOP OF
CANNON

CUT 2 BLACK

CUT 2 RED

CANNON
BALL
CUT 2
BLACK

BOTTOM OF CANNON
1ST HALF
CUT 2

BLUE STRIPE

CUT 2
RED

CUT 2
BLACK

CUT 2
GOLD

When the reality of the war between the Northern and Southern states became clear, women began sewing quilts and comforts for the men and boys who signed up to fight. The Sanitary Commission asked that the quilts be made long and narrow so they could easily be rolled up and carried in a bedroll. The sizes varied but were approximately 56″ x 76″.

Since this is a random scrappy quilt, such as the original soldier's quilts probably were, choose flannels or woven fabrics in checks and plaids, and stripes. You will want a good variety of lights and darks, with a few mediums added. This quilt may be sewn quickly, quilted with a simple "in the ditch" method or tied as a comfort. Women produced these quilts quickly, so no fancy quilting or complicated pieced work.

SOLDIER'S STRIPPY QUILT

55″ X 76″

Yardage

- 2 ½ yards light and 2 ½ yards dark woven fabrics or Civil War era reproduction calico prints

- 2 ⅓ yards woven stripe or ticking for the borders

Cutting and Sewing Directions

These measurements include ¼″ seam allowance.

For 28 - 10″ Four Patch Variation blocks:

- Cut 56 light 5 ⅞″ squares. Cut on the diagonal for 112 light triangles. *See Figure 1.*

- Cut 56 dark 5 ⅞″ squares. Cut on the diagonal for 112 dark triangles. *See Figure 1.*

Piecing blocks together

- Create 28 Four Patch Variation blocks referring to *Figure 2* for color placement and assembling. Sew 7 blocks into 4 separate vertical rows.

Borders

Measure your set block rows and cut borders to fit your row length.

- Cut 5 - 3 ½″ x 70 ½″ lengths of woven fabric for vertical strips.

- Refer to *Figure 3* to assemble quilt. Begin on the left side of quilt and sew 1 border strip to the left side of vertical block row 1. Sew another strip to the right side of block row 1. Repeat block rows and strips ending with a woven border on the right side of the quilt.

- Measure your quilt width and then cut top and bottom borders to fit.

- Cut 2 - 3 ½″ x 55 ½″ lengths of woven fabric for top and bottom borders.

- Add the top and bottom borders to the quilt.

- Quilt in the ditch or tie into a comfort.

FIG. 3

FIG. 2

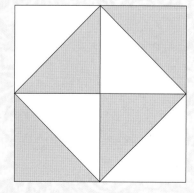

FIG. 1

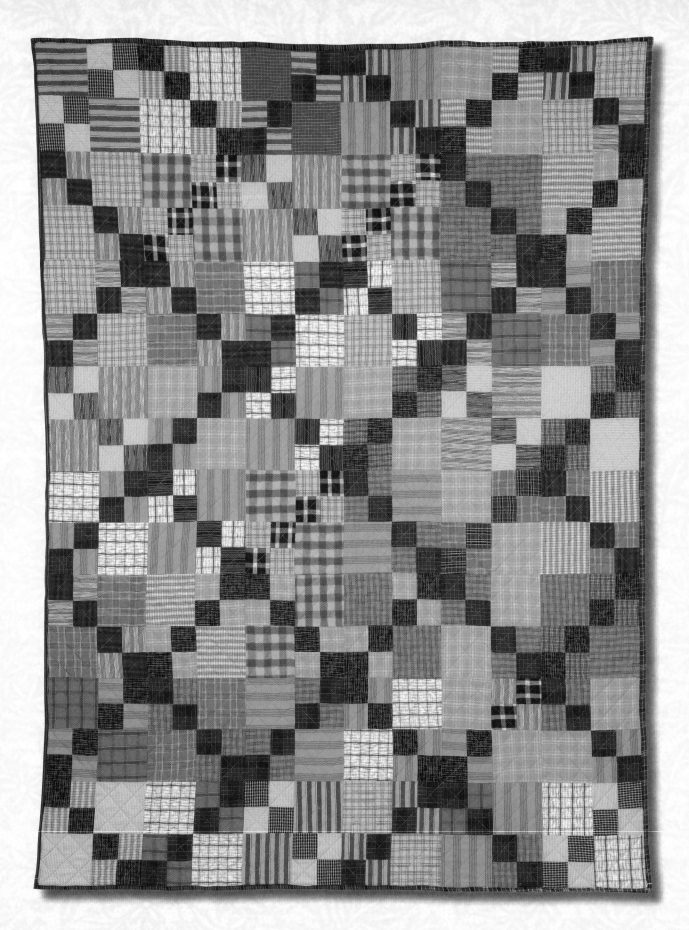

Four Patch Soldier's Quilt

60˝ X 80˝

Yardage

You will want to use a variety of blue, tan and brown in plaids and stripes

- 2 ½ yards neutral fabric for all plain 5″ blocks
- 1 ½ yards light fabric for 5″ Four Patch blocks
- 1 ½ yards dark fabric for 5″ Four Patch blocks

Cutting and Sewing Directions

Measurements include seam allowance.

- Cut 192 light 3″ squares for the Four Patch blocks.
- Cut 192 dark 3″ squares for the Four Patch blocks.
- Cut 96 - 5″ squares for plain blocks.
- Referring to *Figure 1* create 96 Four Patch blocks.
- Referring to *Figure 2* sew the Four Patch blocks to the 5″ plain blocks to create 48 - 10″ Four Patch blocks.
- Refer to *Figure 3* to assemble rows in order to create the chain effect. You will create 8 rows of 6 - 10″ blocks.
- Quilt and bind.

FIG. 1

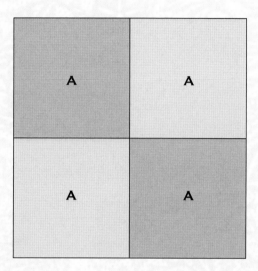

FIG. 2

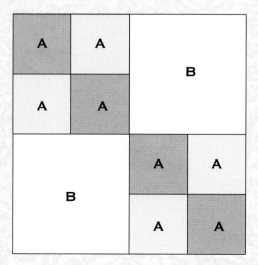

FIG. 3

Suggested Reading

- *A Hunger for Home: Louisa May Alcott's Place in American culture* - Sarah Elbert - Rutgers University Press 1997

- *American Bloomsbury* - Susan Cheever - Simon and Schuster

- *Facts and Fabrications - Unraveling the History of Quilts and Slavery* - Barbara Brackman - C&T Publishing

- *Revolutionary Heart* - Diane Eickoff - Quindaro Press 2006

- *Four Block Quilts: Pieced Boldly and Appliquéd Freely* - Terry Clothier Thompson - Kansas City Star books

- *Dressed for the Photographer* - Joan L. Severa - Kent State University Press 1995

Bibliography

[1] *Louisa May Alcott – Her Life, Letters and Journals* – Louisa May Alcott published 1892 – Boston-Roberts Brothers – Ednah D. Cheney - editor

[2] *Louisa May Alcott* - Martha Saxton - Houghton Mifflin Company 1977 – Noonday press 1995